Interview with the
Guardian Spirit of
U.N. Secretary-General

Ban

潘基文
(バン・キムン)
国連事務総長の
守護霊インタビュー

大川隆法
Ryuho Okawa

Interview with the
Guardian Spirit of
U.N. Secretary-General

Ban

潘基文(バン・キムン)
国連事務総長の
守護霊インタビュー

大川隆法
Ryuho Okawa

本霊言は、2013年10月5日(写真上・下)、幸福の科学総合本部にて、
質問者との対話形式で公開収録された。

# 潘基文国連事務総長の
# 守護霊インタビュー

Interview with the Guardian Spirit of

United Nations Secretary-General

Ban Ki-moon

*Preface*

Sadness might be akin to reality. But reality seldom akin to the fact.

The higher in this world rarely think much of the happiness of the common people. It is the time that true leader should appear. I'd like to expect Japanese Samurai-Spirit. We will be able to do something great in this age. True historical recognition is the Justice of God. This book itself is the judgement from Heaven. This light comes from original universe. Please tell bad from good. Where love is, God is. Where mercy is, Buddha is. Where wisdom is, I am.

October 15, 2013

Master & CEO of Happy Science Group

Ryuho Okawa

# はじめに

　悲しみは何と真実に近いのだろう。しかし真実が事実に似ていることはまれである。
　この世にて高い地位にある者たちが、ありきたりな人々の幸福について深く考えることはまれである。もう真のリーダーが現れなければならない時だ。私は日本人のサムライ精神に期待したい。日本人はこの時代に、何かすごいことがやれると思う。真なる歴史認識とは、神の正義である。この本自体が天上界からの審判である。この光は根源なる宇宙から来ている。
　善と悪とを分かちなさい。愛のあるところ、神はいる。慈悲のあるところ、仏陀はいる。知恵のあるところ、そこに私はいる。

2013 年 10 月 15 日

幸福の科学グループ創始者兼総裁

大川隆法

# Contents

Preface 2

1 Summoning the Guardian Spirit of U.N. Secretary-General Ban 16

2 Guardian Spirit Stresses that His Opinion is Not the Same as Ban's 20

3 The U.N. Has No Power Before America and Russia 32

4 Raison d'Être of Secretary-General is to Gather Funds 48

5 Should the U.N. Security Council Be Expanded? No 62

6 Existence of Japanese People Itself is a Great Disaster of the World 70

7 Guardian Spirit Doesn't Know About World Economy 82

目　次

　はじめに　　3

1　潘国連事務総長の守護霊を招霊する　　17

2　「潘氏本人と意見は同じではない」と強調する守護霊　　21

3　米露の陰で国連は「無力である」　　33

4　事務総長の存在意義は「資金を集めること」　　49

5　安保理常任理事国の拡大は「ノー」　　63

6　日本人の存在自体が「世界の大災害」　　71

7　世界経済のことは「自分には分からない」　　83

8 South Korea and China Must Cooperate
   to Change the Dangerous Japanese Government      88
9 Purpose of Promoting Comfort Women
   Campaign in the U.S.: "Permanent Member
   South Korea"      94
10 The U.N. is Not a Fair Institution from its
   Founding      102
11 We Cannot Criticize America, the Owner
   of the U.N.      112
12 Guardian Spirit: "I Have No Leadership"      120
13 Secretary-General is "Secret General"      128
14 Comparing the Figures: People Kidnapped vs.
   Possible Casualties of a War Between North and
   South Korea      134
15 I am an Adjuster Who Just Thinks About the
   Benefit of South Korea      140
16 Japanese People Should Think About Their Sin or
   Their Fathers' Sin      146
17 The Tie Between Ban and the Unification
   Church      152

8 韓国と中国が協力して日本の「危険な」
　　政府を変えたい　　　　　　　　　　　　89

9 アメリカでの慰安婦問題推進の目的は
　　「韓国が常任理事国になるため」　　　　　95

10 国連は設立当初から「公平な機関ではない」　103

11 国連のオーナーであるアメリカのことは批判で
　　きない　　　　　　　　　　　　　　　　113

12 私にはリーダーシップなんかない　　　　121

13 事務総長とは「秘密総長」である　　　　129

14 拉致人数と、南北朝鮮で戦争が起きた
　　場合の死者数を比較　　　　　　　　　　135

15 私は韓国の利益だけを考えている「調整者」　141

16 日本人は自分たちや父祖の罪を考えよ　　147

17 潘氏と統一協会の関係について　　　　　153

| | |
|---|---:|
| 18 I'm Not a Leader Who Makes Decisions | 160 |
| 19 Mr. Abe Should Destroy Yasukuni Shrine | 166 |
| 20 We Will Never Forgive Japanese People | 172 |
| 21 Past Life: Gandhi, Christ or Buddha? | 180 |
| 22 Guardian Spirit Insists He is Neutral; Next Mission is President of South Korea | 190 |
| 23 After the Interview with the Guardian Spirit of U.N. Secretary-General Ban | 198 |

| 18 | 私は意思決定をするリーダーではない | 161 |
| 19 | 安倍氏は靖国神社を壊すべき | 167 |
| 20 | 我々は決して日本人を許さない | 173 |
| 21 | 過去世は「ガンジーかキリストか仏陀」？ | 181 |
| 22 | あくまで「中立」を主張。次の使命は「韓国大統領」 | 191 |
| 23 | 「潘国連事務総長の守護霊インタビュー」を終えて | 199 |

This book is the transcript of spiritual messages given by the guardian spirit of the United Nations Secretary-General Ban Ki-moon.

These spiritual messages were channeled through Ryuho Okawa. However, please note that because of his high level of enlightenment, his way of receiving spiritual messages is fundamentally different from other psychic mediums who undergo trances and are completely taken over by the spirits they are channeling.

Each human soul is made up of six soul siblings, one of whom acts as the guardian spirit of the person living on earth. People living on earth are connected to their guardian spirits at the innermost subconscious level. They are a part of people's very souls, and therefore, exact reflections of their thoughts and philosophies.

It should be noted that these spiritual messages are opinions of the individual spirits and may contradict the ideas or teachings of the Happy Science Group.

The spiritual messages and questions were spoken in English.

本書は、国連事務総長潘基文の守護霊の霊言を収録したものである。

　「霊言現象」とは、あの世の霊存在の言葉を語り下ろす現象のことをいう。これは高度な悟りを開いた者に特有のものであり、「霊媒現象」（トランス状態になって意識を失い、霊が一方的にしゃべる現象）とは異なる。

　また、人間の魂は６人のグループからなり、あの世に残っている「魂の兄弟」の１人が守護霊を務めている。つまり、守護霊は、実は自分自身の魂の一部である。

　したがって、「守護霊の霊言」とは、いわば、本人の潜在意識にアクセスしたものであり、その内容は、その人が潜在意識で考えていること（本心）と考えてよい。

　ただ、「霊言」は、あくまでも霊人の意見であり、幸福の科学グループとしての見解と矛盾する内容を含む場合がある点、付記しておきたい。

　なお、今回、霊人や質問者の発言は英語にて行われた。本書は、それに日本語訳を付けたものである。

# Interview with the Guardian Spirit of United Nations Secretary-General Ban Ki-moon

October 5, 2013 at Happy Science General Headquarters

Spiritual Messages from the Guardian Spirit of Ban Ki-moon

# 潘基文国連事務総長の
# 守護霊インタビュー

2013年10月5日　幸福の科学総合本部にて
潘基文守護霊の霊言

# Ban Ki-moon (1944~)

The eighth secretary-general of the United Nations. Born in Japanese Korea (currently the Republic of Korea). Graduated with a bachelor's degree in international relations from Seoul National University in 1970 and joined the Ministry of Foreign Affairs that year. Ban earned a master's degree from the John F. Kennedy School of Government at Harvard University in 1985. After serving roles such as U.S.-stationed minister, U.N. ambassador and foreign minister, Ban was elected U.N. secretary-general in October 2006. He is the incumbent secretary-general since January 2007 and is currently serving his second term (which terminates at the end of 2016). Ban has been criticized by the Western media, out of all secretary-generals, as particularly incompetent, and has also been questioned in regard to his neutrality.

### Interviewers

Masashi Ishikawa
  Deputy Chief Secretary, First Secretarial Division
  Religious Affairs Headquarters

Kazuhiro Ichikawa
  Senior Managing Director
  Chief Director of International Headquarters

Yukihisa Oikawa
  Director of Foreign Affairs
  Happiness Realization Party

※ Interviewers are listed in the order that they appear in the transcript.
  Their professional titles represent their positions at the time of the interview.

## 潘基文（パン・キムン）（1944 〜）

第8代国際連合事務総長。日本領朝鮮（現・大韓民国）生まれ。1970年ソウル大学外交学科卒業。同年、外交部（外務省にあたる）に入部。その後ハーバード大学ケネディ行政大学院に留学、1985年修士号取得。駐米公使、国連大使、外交通商部長官（外務大臣）などを経て2006年10月、国連事務総長選挙に立候補し当選。2007年1月より現職。現在2期目（2016年末まで）を務めるが、欧米メディアなどから「歴代事務総長のなかでも際立って無能」と批判され、中立性に疑問を呈されることも少なくない。

### 質問者

石川雅士（いしかわまさし）（幸福の科学宗務本部第一秘書局担当局長）
市川和博（いちかわかずひろ）（幸福の科学専務理事　兼　国際本部長）
及川幸久（おいかわゆきひさ）（幸福実現党外務局長）

※質問順。役職は収録当時のもの

# 1 Summoning the Guardian Spirit of U.N. Secretary-General Ban

**Ryuho Okawa** Today I would like to summon Mr. Ban Ki-moon, the secretary-general of the U.N. He has a lot of problems now so we'd like to ask him about his real thinking, decisions and direction. We'd like to ask him about that.

But, maybe he wouldn't like to be asked about that because he is in a high position, the highest position. If we fail to catch his real thinking, we will get almost nothing from him.

So be wise and be clever and ask him as if you were a diplomat. Maybe he has some weak points, so please hit those points and please induce from him his real thinking about Japan and, of course, about other areas of conflict in the world, and his real decisions regarding the great powers of the world, for example, the U.S.A., Russia or China. I hope so.

OK, anyway, I will try. In New York, it's late

# 1　潘国連事務総長の守護霊を招霊する

大川隆法　今日は、潘基文国連事務総長を招霊したいと思います。彼は現在、多くの問題を抱えていますので、その本心、判断、方向性などを伺いたいと思います。そのようなことを伺いたいと思います。

　ただ、おそらく彼は、その高い立場、最高の立場ゆえに、それについては聞かれたくないでしょう。もし、本心をつかむことに失敗すれば、彼からはほとんど何も得ることはできないでしょう。

　ですから、賢く、上手に、外交官のように聞いてください。弱点もあるでしょうから、その点を突いて、日本や、もちろん世界の他の紛争地域についての彼の考えや、世界の大国に対する本当のところの判断などについて、その本心を引き出してください。例えば、アメリカやロシア、中国のような国です。それを期待しています。

　よろしいですか。とにかく、やってみます。現在、ニュー

night now, maybe. So, I guess he will say, "I'm very busy" and want to run away from the Happy Science headquarters. But please catch him, OK?

Then, I'd like to summon the guardian spirit of Mr. Ban Ki-moon, the secretary-general of the U.N. Mr. Ban Ki-moon, Mr. Ban Ki-moon, come over here to Japan. Come over here to Tokyo. We are Happy Science, a religious group, and we want to ask you about foreign affairs. Could you tell us, Japanese people, about your real meaning regarding the activities of the U.N.? Mr. Ban Ki-moon, the guardian spirit of Ban Ki-moon, Mr. Ban, come down here, please.

## 1　潘国連事務総長の守護霊を招霊する

ヨークは夜遅いでしょう。おそらく彼は、「私は非常に忙しいんだ」と言って、この幸福の科学の総合本部から逃げ出したがると思いますが、どうか、彼をつかまえてください。よろしいでしょうか。

　それでは、国連事務総長である潘基文氏の守護霊を招霊したいと思います。潘基文氏、潘基文氏、どうか、ここ、日本にお越しください。ここ、東京にお越しください。私たちは、幸福の科学という宗教団体で、外交問題についてお尋ねしたいと思います。私たち日本人に、国連の活動についての本当のところを語っていただけますでしょうか。潘基文氏よ、潘基文の守護霊よ、潘氏よ、どうか、こちらに降りてきてください。

## 2 Guardian Spirit Stresses that His Opinion is Not the Same as Ban's

(About 14 seconds of silence)

**Ban's Guardian Spirit*** Mmm… mmm…

**Ishikawa** Good morning.

**Ban's G.S.** Japan?

**Ishikawa** Yes. In Tokyo.

**Ban's G.S.** Japan? Japan? Japan? Japana? Japana?

**Ishikawa** Yes, Japanese, yes.

**Ban's G.S.** Japan?

*Ban's Guardian Spirit will be noted as Ban's G.S. from this point on.

## 2 「潘氏本人と意見は同じではない」と強調する守護霊

(約14秒間の沈黙)

潘守護霊　うーん、うーん。

石川　おはようございます。

潘守護霊　日本か？

石川　はい、東京です。

潘守護霊　日本？　日本？　日本？　ジャパーナ？　ヤパーナ？

石川　はい、日本人です。そうです。

潘守護霊　日本？

## 2 Guardian Spirit Stresses that His Opinion is Not the Same as Ban's

**Ishikawa** Yes.

**Ban's G.S.** *Nippon?*

**Ishikawa** Are you the guardian spirit of Ban Ki-moon?

**Ban's G.S.** Uh huh. Yes.

**Ishikawa** Today, we would like to have a spiritual interview with you because you are the secretary-general of the U.N....

**Ban's G.S.** Ohh.

**Ishikawa** So everyone wants to know your true intentions.

**Ban's G.S.** Spiritual interview?

## 2 「潘氏本人と意見は同じではない」と強調する守護霊

石川　そうです。

潘守護霊　ニッポン？

石川　あなたは、潘基文の守護霊でいらっしゃいますか。

潘守護霊　うん、そうだけど。

石川　本日は、守護霊インタビューを行わせていただきたいと思います。というのも、あなたは、国連事務総長であられますから……。

潘守護霊　おお。

石川　ですから、誰もが、あなたの本心を知りたがっているのです。

潘守護霊　守護霊インタビューかい？

## 2 Guardian Spirit Stresses that His Opinion is Not the Same as Ban's

**Ishikawa**  Yes, yes.

**Ban's G.S.**  Huh! It's my first trial.

**Ishikawa**  Yes, first trial.

**Ban's G.S.**  Uh huh… Incredible!

**Ishikawa**  Yeah, yeah, yeah.

**Ban's G.S.**  What's this? Could you explain about this spiritual interview? What is this?

**Ishikawa**  Yes. First of all, do you know Happy Science?

**Ban's G.S.**  No. Or, a little, yes.

**Ishikawa**  A little, yes?

## 2 「潘氏本人と意見は同じではない」と強調する守護霊

石川　ええ、そうです。

潘守護霊　フン！　初めての試みだな。

石川　ええ、初めての試みです。

潘守護霊　そうだな。信じられない！

石川　ええ、ええ、ええ。

潘守護霊　これ、何なんだ？　この守護霊インタビューというのを説明してくれんかね。これは何なんだ？

石川　はい。まず、幸福の科学はご存じでしょうか。

潘守護霊　いや。あ、少しは知ってる。

石川　少しご存じですか。

## 2 Guardian Spirit Stresses that His Opinion is Not the Same as Ban's

**Ban's G.S.** But, almost no.

**Ishikawa** So, according to Happy Science teachings, we are spiritual beings.

**Ban's G.S.** Uh huh.

**Ishikawa** We all have souls and each of us…

**Ban's G.S.** OK, OK.

**Ishikawa** …has a guardian spirit.

**Ban's G.S.** OK, OK, I agree.

**Ishikawa** Yes. So, if we can ask the guardian spirit, we can hear your true intentions.

**Ban's G.S.** Hmm… true intentions or true tension? Oh, I don't know.

## 2 「潘氏本人と意見は同じではない」と強調する守護霊

**潘守護霊** でも、ほとんど知らないな。

**石川** そうですね。幸福の科学の教えによれば、私たちは霊的な存在です。

**潘守護霊** うん。

**石川** 私たちには魂(たましい)があり、一人ひとりに……。

**潘守護霊** 分かった、分かった。

**石川** 守護霊がついています。

**潘守護霊** 分かった、分かった。その通り。

**石川** はい。それで、もし、守護霊に聞くことができれば、あなたの本心を聞くことができるというわけです。

**潘守護霊** んー、本心なのか、本当のテンションなのか、知らんけどな。

## 2 Guardian Spirit Stresses that His Opinion is Not the Same as Ban's

**Ishikawa**  Yes. For example, we conducted a spiritual interview with Assad.

**Ban's G.S.**  Assad?

**Ishikawa**  The Syrian president.

**Ban's G.S.**  I am different from him. Quite different. I am a peacemaker.

**Ishikawa**  Yes, so all politicians have a public stance and maybe they can't express their own intentions or true opinions, so perhaps you also have a public stance and your own opinion, your true opinion.

**Ban's G.S.**  First of all, I'd like to say that my opinion or the guardian spirit's opinion and Mr. Ban, the real Mr. Ban's opinion are not the same. It depends on the question. He himself thinks through his brain and he's seeking for the right answer. But I am the guardian

## 2 「潘氏本人と意見は同じではない」と強調する守護霊

石川　はい。例えば、私たちはアサドの守護霊インタビューを行いました。

潘守護霊　アサド？

石川　シリアの大統領です。

潘守護霊　私は彼とは違うよ。全然違う。私は調停者だ。

石川　ええ、政治家は誰でも公的立場がありますので、おそらく、本心や本当の意見が言えないのだと思います。ですから、あなたにも、公的立場と、あなたご自身の意見、本当の意見とがおありなのではないかと思います。

潘守護霊　まず言っておきたいのは、私の意見、つまり守護霊の意見と、潘氏の、実際の潘氏の意見は、同じではないということだ。質問にもよるけどね。彼自身は頭脳で考えて、正しい答えを模索しているが、私は守護霊だ。もちろん、彼にインスピレーションは送っているけ

spirit. I, of course, give him some inspiration but he sometimes misunderstands my inspiration, so it's not the same. First of all, I must stress this point.

**Ishikawa**  OK. I see.

**Ban's G.S.**  All right?

**Ishikawa**  Then are you ready?

**Ban's G.S.**  Mm… not ready but… *bochi-bochi ne*.

**Ishikawa**  (laughs) OK.

**Ban's G.S.**  OK?

れども、彼はそのインスピレーションを時々誤解するから、同じではない。最初に、この点を強調しておかないといけない。

石川　分かりました。

潘守護霊　大丈夫(だいじょうぶ)かな？

石川　では、よろしいでしょうか。

潘守護霊　んー、よろしくはないが……。ボチボチね。

石川　（笑）分かりました。

潘守護霊　いいかな？

# 3 The U.N. Has No Power Before America and Russia

**Ishikawa**  I think the U.N. has many important roles. For example, the maintenance of peace and security, promotion of disarmament, human rights protection and humanitarian assistance…

**Ban's G.S.**  Ohh… it's OK, OK. Enough, enough, enough, enough. OK. I know about the U.N. OK, OK.

**Ishikawa**  But recently, with regard to the Syrian issue…

**Ban's G.S.**  Ah, the Syrian issue, OK.

**Ishikawa**  Mr. Putin upstaged the importance of the U.N., so it's not like *hiki-wake*. It was *ippon-gachi*.

## 3　米露の陰で国連は「無力である」

**石川**　国連は、多くの重要な役割を担っていると思います。例えば、平和及び安全の維持、軍縮の推進、人権保護、人道援助……。

**潘守護霊**　おお、分かった、分かった。もういいよ。十分、十分、もう十分だ。もういい。国連については分かっている。いいよ、もういい。

**石川**　しかし、最近、シリア問題に関して……。

**潘守護霊**　ああ、シリア問題ね。

**石川**　プーチン氏が、国連の重要性を出し抜いて、引き分けのようなものではなく、一本勝ちを収めました。

## 3 The U.N. Has No Power Before America and Russia

**Ban's G.S.**  Oh, oh!

**Ishikawa**  I think now the U.N. has little presence in the international community because of superpowers like America and Russia. Could you tell us about that? I think it's a very difficult task, so…

**Ban's G.S.**  Could I ask you one question?

**Ishikawa**  Yes.

**Ban's G.S.**  Are you my enemies or not?

**Ishikawa**  Hmm… it depends on your answer.

**Ban's G.S.**  Depends on… (audience laughs) OK. First, you want to ask about the Syria problem?

**Ishikawa**  Yes, for example, yes.

**潘守護霊**　おお、おお！

石川　現在、国際社会においては、アメリカ、ロシアなどの大国のせいで、国連は存在感が薄くなっていると思います。それについて、お聞かせいただけますでしょうか。非常に難しい仕事だとは思うのですが……。

**潘守護霊**　一つ聞いてもいいかな？

石川　はい。

**潘守護霊**　君たちは、敵か、味方か？

石川　うーん、それはあなたの答えによります。

**潘守護霊**　答えによるか（会場笑）。分かった。まず、シリア問題について聞きたいわけね？

石川　ええ。例えば、そうです。

## 3 The U.N. Has No Power Before America and Russia

**Ban's G.S.** For example, Syrian... We have no power over that. It's the reality. If Russia and the U.S. want to fight a battle about the Syrian problem, we can do nothing.

**Ishikawa** I see.

**Ban's G.S.** And I myself will be nothing at that time.

**Ishikawa** I have another question. For example, in 2010, I think...

**Ban's G.S.** Uh huh. 2010? OK.

**Ishikawa** Yes. A North Korean submarine sank South Korea's warship.

**Ban's G.S.** Ohh... (laughs).

**潘守護霊** 例えば、シリアの……。それに関しては、我々は無力なんだよ。それが現実だね。ロシアとアメリカがシリア問題を巡って争いたいなら、我々にできることなんて何もない。

**石川** なるほど。

**潘守護霊** そして、そうなれば私自身が、何者でもなくなってしまう。

**石川** では、もう一つ伺います。例えば、2010年だと思いますが……。

**潘守護霊** うん。2010年？ どうぞ。

**石川** ええ。北朝鮮の潜水艦が、韓国の哨戒艦を沈めました。

**潘守護霊** おお……（笑）。

## 3 The U.N. Has No Power Before America and Russia

**Ishikawa** (laughs) Of course, you are the secretary-general of the U.N. but you are also a Korean politician and a South Korean citizen, right? So, in your opinion, perhaps you want to support South Korea, and you want to say to North Korea, "You are a liar."

**Ban's G.S.** Ohh (laughs). You are a bad guy. A bad guy.

**Ishikawa** No, I'm not a bad guy.

**Ban's G.S.** No, no (laughs).

**Ishikawa** But I think that maybe your stance needs to be neutral.

**Ban's G.S.** Ohh (laughs).

**Ishikawa** So I want to ask you about that.

石川　（笑）当然、あなたは国連事務総長ですが、同時に韓国の政治家であり、韓国民ですよね。ですから、あなたのお考えでは、韓国を支持したいのではないでしょうか。そして、北朝鮮を「この嘘つきめ」と呼びたいのではないでしょうか。

潘守護霊　おお（笑）。君は嫌な人だねえ。嫌な人だ。

石川　いいえ、嫌な人ではありません。

潘守護霊　いや、いや（笑）。

石川　しかし、あなたの立場としては、中立が求められるのではないかと思うのですが。

潘守護霊　おお（笑）。

石川　それについて、伺いたいのです。

## 3 The U.N. Has No Power Before America and Russia

**Ban's G.S.** Ohh... Japanese people are bad people.

**Ishikawa** Not bad people. They're fair.

**Ban's G.S.** You're planning to kill me.

**Ishikawa** No, no, no, no.

**Ban's G.S.** In the spiritual meaning, you want to kill me, right?

**Ishikawa** No, no, no, no.

**Ban's G.S.** The issue of South Korea and North Korea is a very difficult matter.

**Ishikawa** Yes, yes.

**Ban's G.S.** Of course, I like South Korea, of course, but I cannot say that because I'm the secretary-

**潘守護霊** おお、日本人ってのは、ひどい国民だなあ。

**石川** ひどい国民ではありません。公平です。

**潘守護霊** 君は、私を殺すつもりだな。

**石川** いえいえ、違います。

**潘守護霊** 霊的(れいてき)には、殺したいんだろう？

**石川** いえいえ、そうではありません。

**潘守護霊** 韓国と北朝鮮は、非常に難しい問題なんだよ。

**石川** ええ、そうですね。

**潘守護霊** もちろん、私は韓国が好きだよ。当たり前だろう。だが、それを言うことはできない。だって、私は

general. So I am generous. I must have a general thinking about the world. So, it is a little difficult to answer, but maybe North is always bad.

**Ishikawa** Bad.

**Ban's G.S.** Mm…

**Ishikawa** I see. Is that your opinion?

**Ban's G.S.** Yeah. But it's a top secret, right? Secret.

**Ishikawa** It's a little different from Ban Ki-moon's opinion.

**Ban's G.S.** It's a little secret.

**Ishikawa** A little secret. I see. So, I think in 2006, you were chosen as the secretary-general of the U.N.

事務総長だからね。だから私は寛大(かんだい)なのよ。世界について、総合的に考えなければならない。だから、ちょっと答えるのが難しいんだけど、北は常に悪いだろうね。

石川　悪いですか。

潘守護霊　うん。

石川　分かりました。それがあなたのご意見ですね。

潘守護霊　そう。でも、最高機密だからね。いいかな？　秘密だよ。

石川　それは、潘基文の意見とは少し違いますね。


潘守護霊　ちょっとした秘密なんだよ。

石川　ちょっとした秘密ですか。分かりました。では、2006年だったと思いますが、あなたは国連の事務総長に

and at that time, initially, you were considered to be a long shot for the office.

**Ban's G.S.** (does a golf swing)

**Ishikawa** Yes. The other candidates were regarded as better candidates. But in the end you became the front-runner and you were chosen. So how was the Korean government involved in the lobbying activities? Is it possible for you to answer this?

**Ban's G.S.** Oh, you have (clicks tongue) hmm... a slightly bad nature. You should change your character and be a moderate person. You should try.

**Ishikawa** OK, I will try. But please answer my question.

**Ban's G.S.** If you want to become a public person,

選ばれました。当時、あなたは当初、その職務に就ける見込みはない(ロング・ショット)だろうと目されていました。

潘守護霊　(ゴルフのスウィングの格好をする)

石川　ええ。他の候補者たちのほうが、より優れた候補者と見られていました。しかし最終的に、あなたが最有力候補となり、選ばれました。そこで、韓国政府は、どのようにロビー活動に関わっていたのでしょうか。お答えいただけますでしょうか。

潘守護霊　おお、君は(舌打ち)、うーん、ちょっと性格が悪いよ。性格を変えたほうがいい。穏健な人間にならないといかん。そう心がけたほうがいいよ。

石川　分かりました。やってみます。ただ、どうか質問にお答えください。

潘守護霊　公人になりたいなら、穏健になれよ。

be moderate.

**Ishikawa** Yes. I forgot if it was last month or not, but you visited South Korea.

**Ban's G.S.** Yes.

**Ishikawa** Yes. And I think you said, "Japan needs to have a correct historical view" and you were criticized.

**Ban's G.S.** Ohh, I know, I know. I know your intention.

**Ishikawa** (laughs)

**Ban's G.S.** This is the most difficult question. I must run away from this question.

**Ishikawa** (laughs) No, no. Please don't run away.

石川　はい。先月だったか忘れてしまいましたが、あなたは韓国を訪問しましたね。

潘守護霊　うん。

石川　ええ。そして、「日本は正しい歴史観を持つ必要がある」とおっしゃったと思います。そして、批判されました。

潘守護霊　おお、分かった、分かった。君の意図はわかったぞ。

石川　（笑）

潘守護霊　これは、いちばん難しい質問だ。この質問からは逃げないといけない。

石川　（笑）いえいえ、どうか、お逃げにならないでください。

**Ban's G.S.**  Oh, I should run away from here (laughs)!

**Ishikawa**  (laughs)

**Ban's G.S.**  Why am I here? I have no obligation to sit here. Can I go back to New York?

# 4 Raison d'Être of Secretary-General is to Gather Funds

**Ishikawa**  I may be a bad person so please... (points to Ichikawa)

**Ichikawa**  Please be a little patient.

**Ban's G.S.**  I'm very busy. A busy, busy person, you know?

**Ichikawa**  We would appreciate it if you could spare some time for us. It's just a short interview.

**潘守護霊** おお、ここから逃げないといかん！（笑）

石川 （笑）

**潘守護霊** なぜ私はここにいるんだ？ ここに座っている義務はない。ニューヨークに帰ってもいいかな。

## 4　事務総長の存在意義は「資金を集めること」

石川 私は悪い人間かもしれませんので、どうぞ……（市川氏を指して）。

市川 どうか、もう少し我慢してください。

**潘守護霊** 私はすごく忙しいんだ。忙しい忙しい人間なんだ。分かる？

市川 私たちのためにお時間を割いていただければ、ありがたく存じます。ほんの短いインタビューですので。

**Ban's G.S.**  Why me?

**Ichikawa**  We are very interested in the world crises. We really admire your opinions about world issues. So I would like to ask you several questions. First, I want to ask you some basic questions.

**Ban's G.S.**  Basic questions?

**Ichikawa**  Yes. What do you think is the raison d'être or function of the secretary-general of the U.N.?

**Ban's G.S.**  Secretary-general? Ohh!

**Ichikawa**  What is your role?

**Ban's G.S.**  Oh, you also want to kill me, huh? (audience laughs)

**Ichikawa**  I won't kill you, so...

## 4　事務総長の存在意義は「資金を集めること」

潘守護霊　なぜ私が？

市川　私たちは、世界の危機に非常に関心がありまして。世界的な問題に対するあなたのご意見に、大変、敬服しています。ですから、いくつか質問させていただきたいのです。まず、基本的な質問をしたいと思います。

潘守護霊　基本的な質問？

市川　はい。国連事務総長の存在意義と申しますか、職務とは、どのようなものであるとお考えでしょうか。

潘守護霊　事務総長？　おお！

市川　あなたの役割は何でしょうか。

潘守護霊　おお、君も私を殺したいんだな？（会場笑）

市川　殺したりしませんので……。

**Ban's G.S.** This question itself is a dynamite for me! Ahh, the raison d'être of the secretary-general... ohh!

**Ichikawa** Or the functions.

**Ban's G.S.** Ohh, I must gather funds from all over the world, so I must be the symbol of the U.N. So I must be a great, smart and respectable person. This is the raison d'être of the secretary-general (laughs). I'm a fund-maker. Sorry about that (laughs).

**Ichikawa** Thank you. So, just recently...

**Ban's G.S.** I'm not a decision-maker. Sorry, sorry. Ohh! (audience laughs) (to Oikawa) His face! Funny.

**Oikawa** OK, let me ask a simple question.

**Ban's G.S.** Simple? OK.

## 4　事務総長の存在意義は「資金を集めること」

**潘守護霊**　この質問自体が、私にとってはダイナマイトだ！　ああ、事務総長の存在意義……。おお！

**市川**　あるいは、職務でも結構です。

**潘守護霊**　おお、私は世界中から資金を集めないといけないんだ。だから、国連のシンボルでなけりゃいけないんだよ。偉大で、賢くて、尊敬すべき人間でなければならない。これが事務総長の存在意義だ（笑）。私は、資金を募る人間なんだよ。申し訳ないけどね（笑）。

**市川**　ありがとうございます。そこで、最近……。

**潘守護霊**　私は、意思決定者じゃないんだよ。すまん、すまん。おお！（会場笑）（及川氏に）彼の顔！　面白いね。

**及川**　では。簡単な質問をさせてください。

**潘守護霊**　簡単な？　いいよ。

**Oikawa**  OK? A simple question.

**Ban's G.S.**  Simple is better.

**Oikawa**  Going back to our conversation about you becoming the secretary-general of the U.N., was it your personal desire to become the secretary-general or was it a strategy of the Korean government?

**Ban's G.S.**  Oh, you, Japanese people… why do you ask such kind of questions?

**Oikawa**  I was just wondering if you wanted to become the secretary-general yourself, or if it was somebody else.

**Ban's G.S.**  I didn't ask for anything. Only God asked me to become the secretary-general. That's the reason.

及川　よろしいですか？　簡単な質問です。

潘守護霊　簡単な方がいいね。

及川　国連の事務総長になられた件に戻りますが、事務総長になるのは、あなたの個人的な願いだったのでしょうか。それとも、韓国政府の戦略だったのでしょうか。

潘守護霊　おお、君たち日本人は……。なんで、そんな質問をするわけ？

及川　単に、どうなのかなと思っただけです。あなたご自身が事務総長になりたかったのか、他の誰かがならせたかったのか。

潘守護霊　私は何も頼んでないよ。神が、私に「事務総長になれ」とおっしゃったまでだ。それが理由だ。

**Ichikawa**  Did you say, "God"?

**Ban's G.S.**  God, yes. God, God, God.

**Ichikawa**  Does that mean you believe in God?

**Ban's G.S.**  Oh, no. This is a bad situation (laughs). (audience laughs) I'm in a bad situation. You are a religious group so (laughs)… Oh, no, no, no, no. All the people in the world asked me to become the secretary-general because I'm a moderate and a very peaceful-minded person, so I'm suitable to be the secretary-general. And I'm not from the greater countries. Korea is a very good country in the world so…

**Oikawa**  However, a Korean secretary-general is very unique in the history of the United Nations because Korea has many, as you know, conflicts with other countries, right? However, normally, the U.N. should

## 4　事務総長の存在意義は「資金を集めること」

市川　「神」とおっしゃいましたか。

潘守護霊　神、そうだ。神、神、神だよ。

市川　神を信じていらっしゃるということでしょうか。

潘守護霊　ああ、しまった。まずい状況だ（笑）。（会場笑）まずい状況になったな。君たちは宗教団体だから（笑）……。おお、しまった。違う、違う、違う。世界中の人が、私に事務総長になって欲しいと頼んだんだよ。何しろ、私は穏健で、非常に平和的な心の人間だからね。だから、事務総長にふさわしいわけだよ。大国の出身でもないしね。韓国は、世界の中でも非常にいい国だから……。

及川　しかし、韓国人の事務総長というのは国連史上、非常に珍しいと思います。というのも、韓国は、ご存じの通り、他国といろいろ対立していますから。そうですよね？　しかし通常、国連は中立でなければなりません。

be neutral, so that's why the U.N. doesn't choose any leaders from such kind of countries. So, why did they choose a Korean secretary-general as a world leader this time? We were wondering why.

**Ban's G.S.** Of course, I suggest that you, Japanese people, should choose one suitable person to become the secretary-general. But the Japanese people are hated by the other countries of the world and Japanese people cannot speak English like you. I say this in a good meaning. But Japanese politicians in higher positions cannot speak English, so even a suitable person cannot become the secretary-general of the U.N. So you should make efforts to become the secretary-general.

**Oikawa** Thank you.

**Ban's G.S.** You should.

だからこそ、国連は、そういった国からリーダーを選ぶことはないのです。なぜ今回、韓国人が、世界のリーダーとしての事務総長になったのでしょうか。それが不思議なんです。

**潘守護霊** もちろん、君たち日本人だって、事務総長になるのにふさわしい人を誰か一人選んだらいいと思うよ。でも、日本人は世界の国々から嫌わ(きら)れているし、日本人は君みたいには英語が話せないからね。これはいい意味で言ってるんだよ。でも、日本の政府高官は英語が話せないから、ふさわしい人でも、国連の事務総長にはなれないのよ。君が努力して事務総長になったらいいだろう。

**及川** ありがとうございます。

**潘守護霊** 努力するべきだよ。

**Oikawa**  Thank you. Do you think you are suitable to be secretary-general?

**Ban's G.S.**  Oh, no, no. I'm a very good person so I don't ever say such kind of words. That's the reason I became the secretary-general.

**Ishikawa**  Yeah. But China has a veto right, so it is very difficult for Japanese to choose the...

**Ban's G.S.**  Ah, China.

**Ishikawa**  Yes, yes.

**Ban's G.S.**  China.

**Ishikawa**  Yes. You know very well.

**Ban's G.S.**  Ah, the China problem.

及川　ありがとうございます。あなたは、ご自分が事務総長にふさわしいとお思いですか。

潘守護霊　いやいや、私は非常に人がいいからね。絶対そんなことは言わないよ。そういう理由で、事務総長になったんだから。

石川　そうですね。しかし、中国が拒否権を持っていますので、日本人が選ぶのは非常に難しいと……。

潘守護霊　ああ、中国ね。

石川　ええ、そうです。

潘守護霊　中国。

石川　ええ、よくご存じだと思います。

潘守護霊　ああ、中国問題ね。

**Ishikawa**  Yes, yes.

**Ban's G.S.**  (clicks tongue) China, China, China, China, China, China…

# 5 Should the U.N. Security Council Be Expanded? No

**Ishikawa**  OK, I want to ask you from a different angle. OK?

**Ban's G.S.**  OK.

**Ishikawa**  So now, the U.S. is gradually stepping down from its role of policing the world.

**Ban's G.S.**  It's a top secret. Shh.

**Ishikawa**  Top secret? For example…

石川　ええ、そうです。

潘守護霊　（舌打ち）中国、中国、中国、中国、中国、中国……。

## 5　安保理常任理事国の拡大は「ノー」

石川　では、別の角度からお聞きしたいと思います。よろしいでしょうか。

潘守護霊　どうぞ。

石川　現在アメリカは、少しずつ世界の警察の役割から下りようとしています。

潘守護霊　それは最高機密だ。シーッ。

石川　最高機密ですか？　例えば……。

## 5 Should the U.N. Security Council Be Expanded? No

**Ban's G.S.**  Never, never, never say that.

**Ishikawa**  In that sense, maybe you need a U.N. reform or U.N. transformation. Should the U.N. Security Council be expanded? What are your thoughts or comments on this?

**Ban's G.S.**  Hmm.

**Ishikawa**  For example, Japan, Brazil or Germany...

**Ban's G.S.**  Ah, no. No, no, no, no.

**Ishikawa**  Should they join the Security Council as permanent members? Is it effective?

**Ban's G.S.**  We have, as you know, five permanent members, but even if it is only five countries, they cannot cooperate. So it's very difficult to manage the U.N. So if Japan or Germany joins as a permanent

## 5　安保理常任理事国の拡大は「ノー」

**潘守護霊**　それは絶対、絶対、絶対、言っちゃ駄目だ。

**石川**　その意味でも、国連改革、国連変革が必要かと思いますが、国連の安全保障理事会は、拡大すべきでしょうか。これに関して、あなたのお考えやコメントは？

**潘守護霊**　うーん。

**石川**　例えば、日本やブラジル、ドイツなど……。

**潘守護霊**　ああ、駄目だね。駄目、駄目、駄目、駄目。

**石川**　そういった国々が常任理事国として安保理に加わるべきではないでしょうか。効果はあるでしょうか。

**潘守護霊**　国連には知っての通り、5つの常任理事国があるけれども、たったの5カ国でさえ協力できないでいる。だから、国連を運営するのは非常に難しいんだよ。もし日本やドイツが常任理事国に加わったら複雑になるし、

member, it will become complicated, and India, also, very difficult. No one can manage the Security Council.

**Ishikawa** Additionally, I think the secretary-general of the U.N. is not chosen from the Security Council permanent members, right?

**Ban's G.S.** Yeah, yeah, yeah, yeah.

**Ishikawa** For example, from China. So, I think its role or influence is very limited.

**Ban's G.S.** From neutral countries.

**Ishikawa** From the African countries or...

**Ban's G.S.** So, a minor country. In another meaning, a foreign minister of a minor country.

**Ishikawa** So...

さらにインドもとなると、実に難しい。誰も安全保障理事会を運営できなくなるよ。

石川　さらに、国連の事務総長は、安全保障理事会の常任理事国からは選ばれないことになっていると思いますが、そうですよね？

潘守護霊　そう、そう、そう、そう。

石川　例えば、中国などからは。ですから、その役割や影響は、非常に限られていると思います。

潘守護霊　中立国からだからね。

石川　アフリカの諸国からとか。

潘守護霊　つまり、小国だよ。別の意味から言えば、小国の外務大臣だ。

石川　ですから……。

**Ban's G.S.**  The secretary-general never has enough power to persuade great nations so it's a problem. A problem.

**Ishikawa**  For example, Former Secretary-General Annan was anti-America as it was the case in the Iraq War, so that's why Bush or Condoleezza Rice supported you because you will obey American intentions, American orders.

**Ban's G.S.**  But your intentions are evil.

**Ishikawa**  No, they are not evil. It's a fair question.

**Ban's G.S.**  I'll never resign. This is my calling and I will never say anything to bad questions. I'm very, very busy. Everyone is waiting.

5　安保理常任理事国の拡大は「ノー」

**潘守護霊**　事務総長は、大国を説得するだけの力が充分にあったためしがないから、それが問題なんだ。問題だな。

**石川**　例えば、アナン前事務総長はイラク戦争のこともあって反米的だったので、ブッシュやコンドリーザ・ライスは、あなたを支持したのだと思います。あなたであれば、アメリカの意図、アメリカの命令に従うからです。

**潘守護霊**　でも、君の意図には、良からぬものがあるんじゃないか。

**石川**　いいえ、良からぬことはありません。公平な質問です。

**潘守護霊**　私は絶対、辞任はしないよ。これは私の天命だし、悪い質問に対しては、絶対、何も言わんからな。私はすごくすごく、忙しいんだ。皆が待ってるんだ。

# 6 Existence of Japanese People Itself is a Great Disaster of the World

**Ichikawa**  So before you go back to New York, we have several questions.

**Ban's G.S.**  One minute or two minutes?

**Ichikawa**  Just… one hour, please (audience laughs).

**Ban's G.S.**  Ohh!

**Ichikawa**  OK? And, so the issue now is…

**Ban's G.S.**  Japanese people are difficult people.

**Ichikawa**  What do you think about Japanese people?

**Ban's G.S.**  Huh?

# 6　日本人の存在自体が「世界の大災害」

市川　ニューヨークにお帰りになる前に、もう少し質問したいのですが。

潘守護霊　1、2分か？

市川　ほんの……1時間ほど、お願いできますか（会場笑）。

潘守護霊　おお！

市川　よろしいでしょうか。現在の問題は……。

潘守護霊　日本人は、難しい国民だなあ。

市川　日本人については、どうお考えでしょうか。

潘守護霊　はぁ？

## 6 Existence of Japanese People Itself is a Great Disaster of the World

**Ichikawa** How do you feel about Japanese people?

**Ban's G.S.** Difficult.

**Ichikawa** Difficult?

**Ban's G.S.** Difficult or different... The existence of Japanese people itself is a great disaster of the world! Oh!

**Ichikawa** Why do you think it's a great disaster?

**Ban's G.S.** Because if there were no Japanese people in the world, the world would be peaceful.

**Ichikawa** But Japan is trying to create world peace so we want to support the U.N.

**Ban's G.S.** Money? Oh, yes.

## 6　日本人の存在自体が「世界の大災害」

市川　日本人に対するあなたの感情は、どのようなものでしょうか。

潘守護霊　難しい。

市川　難しいですか。

潘守護霊　難しいんだか、変わってるんだか……。日本人の存在自体が、世界の大災害だ！　おお！

市川　なぜ、大災害だと思われるのですか。

潘守護霊　なぜなら、世界に日本人がいなければ、世界は平和だからだ。

市川　しかし、日本は世界の平和を築こうとしていますので、国連を支持していきたいのです。

潘守護霊　金か？　ああ、そうだな。

**Ichikawa**  Actually, we financially support the U.N.

**Ban's G.S.**  In the context of money, I mean fundraising, you are very useful, but only in this context.

**Ichikawa**  Or if possible, we'd like to guide you.

**Ban's G.S.**  The problem now is, of course, in the area of the Middle East but another problem is, of course, Japan and Korea, the area around North Korea, South Korea and China. East Asia. So you are some kind of an Atomic Bomb. Hidden Atomic Bombs.

**Ichikawa**  I would like to ask about the Japan-South Korea issue. The first point is the Dokdo (Takeshima) Islands.

## 6　日本人の存在自体が「世界の大災害」

市川　実際、私たちは、財政面で国連を支えています。

潘守護霊　お金に関して言うなら、つまり、資金集めに関して言うなら、君らは役に立ってるよ。でも、その面だけだよな。

市川　あるいは、可能であれば、あなたがたをご指導したいと思っています。

潘守護霊　目下の問題は、当然、中東地域にあるが、もう一つの問題は、もちろん、日本と朝鮮、北朝鮮、韓国、中国あたりの地域だ。東アジアだ。君たちはねえ、一種の原爆みたいなもんなんだよ。隠された原爆。

市川　日本と韓国の問題について伺いたいと思います。最初の点は、独島（竹島）です。

**Ban's G.S.**  Ah, Dokdo?

**Ichikawa**  What do you think about the Dokdo Islands?

**Ban's G.S.**  Dokdo... Dokdo... I guess... I guess... I recommend that you abandon the sovereignty of Dokdo to South Korea. That is a good, peacemaking conduct.

**Ishikawa**  No, no. For example, the Japanese government is trying to demand a judgement.

**Ban's G.S.**  Judgement?

**Ishikawa**  Yes, from the International Court of Justice. This institution is the primary judicial branch of the U.N., right?

**Ban's G.S.**  It's not the U.N.

6　日本人の存在自体が「世界の大災害」

潘守護霊　ああ、独島？

市川　独島については、どうお考えでしょうか。

潘守護霊　独島……独島は……たぶん……たぶん……君たちは、韓国に対して独島の主権を放棄(ほうき)すべきだね。それが善なる、平和をもたらす行為(こうい)だ。

石川　いえいえ、例えば、日本政府は、裁判を起こそうとしています。

潘守護霊　裁判？

石川　ええ。国際司法裁判所によってです。この機関は、国連の主要な司法機関ですよね。

潘守護霊　国連ではないよ。

**Ishikawa** It's not the U.N. itself but a part of the U.N., right?

**Ban's G.S.** Hmm, but I'm Korean so… Koreans choose only one conclusion.

**Ishikawa** But you are the secretary-general. So you need to have a neutral stance.

**Ban's G.S.** Yes, a Korean secretary-general.

**Ishikawa** (laughs) Korean…

**Ban's G.S.** Korean secretary-general.

**Ishikawa** Is it OK?

**Ban's G.S.** Not a Japanese secretary-general.

**Ishikawa** We will publish this interview.

石川　国連そのものではありませんが、国連の一部ですよね。

潘守護霊　うーん、だが、私は韓国人だからさ……。韓国人は一つの結論しか選ばんのだ。

石川　しかし、あなたは事務総長ですよ。ですから、中立の立場である必要があります。

潘守護霊　ああ、「韓国人の」事務総長です。

石川　（笑）韓国人の……。

潘守護霊　「韓国人の」事務総長。

石川　それでいいのでしょうか。

潘守護霊　日本人の事務総長ではない。

石川　このインタビューは、出版しますよ。

**Ban's G.S.** If you want to get Dokdo, please choose a secretary-general from Japan.

**Ishikawa** But maybe China will be against it.

**Ban's G.S.** Yes, so that's the reason you should abandon it (laughs).

**Ichikawa** Dokdo is a territory of Japan.

**Ban's G.S.** Oh, really?

**Ichikawa** Yes. But do you think…

**Ban's G.S.** I don't know, I don't know.

**Ichikawa** Is Dokdo a territory of Korea or Japan?

**Ban's G.S.** Korea, of course. Of course.

## 6　日本人の存在自体が「世界の大災害」

潘守護霊　独島を獲得(かくとく)したいんなら、日本から事務総長を選出してくださいよ。

石川　しかし、中国が反対するでしょう。

潘守護霊　そう。だから、放棄すべきなんだ（笑）。

市川　独島は日本の領土です。

潘守護霊　本当か？

市川　はい。しかし、あなたは……。

潘守護霊　それは知らん。知らないね。

市川　独島は、韓国の領土でしょうか、日本の領土でしょうか。

潘守護霊　もちろん、韓国だよ。当たり前だろう。

**Ichikawa**  Why do you think that?

**Ban's G.S.**  Because I passed the exam answering that question like this (laughs). He (Oikawa) is laughing.

# 7 Guardian Spirit Doesn't Know About World Economy

**Oikawa**  OK, OK, let me ask about Germany. OK?

**Ban's G.S.**  Germany?

**Oikawa**  Yes, if you look at Europe now, without Germany, Europe wouldn't work. However, Germany is not a permanent member of the Security Council. So, together with Japan, Germany should join as a permanent member. What do you think?

市川　なぜ、そう思われるのでしょうか。

潘守護霊　なぜなら、そう答えて試験に受かったからだ（笑）。彼（及川氏）は笑ってるぞ。

## 7　世界経済のことは「自分には分からない」

及川　分かりました。では、ドイツについて伺わせてください。よろしいでしょうか。

潘守護霊　ドイツ？

及川　はい。現在、ヨーロッパを見てみると、ドイツなしではヨーロッパは機能しません。しかし、ドイツは安保理の常任理事国ではありません。ですから、日本と一緒に、ドイツも常任理事国に入るべきです。どう思われますか。

**Ban's G.S.** No, no, no. You should talk more with Germany about the territory problem. For example, Germany agreed that the Senkaku Islands belong to China. They said so. Do you know about that? And you still recommend that they join as permanent members of the U.N.? Is this good for you?

**Oikawa** No, Germany never said that the Senkaku Islands should formally belong to China. Germany just said so in connection with their economic relationship with China. So that was a kind of lip service.

**Ban's G.S.** Lip service or not, I don't know, actually.

**Oikawa** I'm talking about the economic side of Europe. Europe is collapsing. How are you going to save Europe? Can you do it without Germany's power?

## 7　世界経済のことは「自分には分からない」

**潘守護霊**　いやいや、駄目だ。あなたがたは、ドイツと領土問題についてもっと話さないといかんよ。例えばドイツは、尖閣諸島は中国に属すると同意した。そう言ったんだが、それは知ってるかな？　それでも君は、ドイツが国連の常任理事国に入るべきだと薦めるのか。それは、君たちにとっていいことかな？

**及川**　いえ、ドイツは、尖閣諸島が正式に中国に所属するとは言っていません。中国との経済関係があるので、一種のリップ・サービスで言っただけでしょう。

**潘守護霊**　リップ・サービスかどうか、実際のところ、私は知らんね。

**及川**　私はヨーロッパの経済面の話をしているのです。ヨーロッパは今、崩壊しつつあります。どうやってヨーロッパを救うおつもりでしょうか。ドイツの力なしで、できますか。

## 7 Guardian Spirit Doesn't Know About World Economy

**Ban's G.S.**  Hmm… the U.N. is not too involved in the economy. We just need to raise funds from other countries. That's all, so we have no power in the world economy. We have no techniques to control the world economy. It depends on the sectors of other world organizations. For example, the World Bank, IMF or G20. So it's above my control.

**Oikawa**  As you know, such kinds of international organizations also are not functioning at the moment.

**Ban's G.S.**  Yes, I know.

**Oikawa**  So that's why the problem still remains.

**Ban's G.S.**  I know, I know.

**Oikawa**  So, now is the time for the U.N.

**Ban's G.S.**  No, no, no. I was a diplomat. Diplomats

**潘守護霊** うーん、国連は、経済にはあまり関わってないんだよ。ただ他の国々から資金を集める必要があるだけだ。それだけだから、世界経済において、我々に力はない。我々には世界経済をコントロールするだけの技術もないしね。他の国際機関の部門次第だな。例えば、世界銀行とか、IMF（国際通貨基金）とかG20（財務相・中央銀行総裁会議）とか。だから、私の手には負えない。

**及川** ご存じの通り、そういった国際機関も、現時点では機能していません。

**潘守護霊** そうだね、知ってるよ。

**及川** ですから、問題がまだ残ったままなのです。

**潘守護霊** 分かってる、分かってる。

**及川** 今こそ、国連の出番です。

**潘守護霊** いやいや、違う。私は外交官の出だ。外交官

usually don't know about the economy, so please forgive me about that.

# 8 South Korea and China Must Cooperate to Change the Dangerous Japanese Government

**Ishikawa**  And I think, as the secretary-general of the U.N., you need to address human rights.

**Ban's G.S.**  Human rights? Human rights. OK, OK. I know, I know, I know.

**Ishikawa**  Yes, but, for example, when you met Previous President Hu Jintao, you did not mention China's human rights problems.

**Ban's G.S.**  China's human rights problems. It's a very, very, very difficult, classical matter! There are no human rights in China.

は通常、経済のことは分からないんだよ。頼（たの）むから、それについては勘弁（かんべん）してよ。

## 8　韓国と中国が協力して日本の「危険な」政府を変えたい

石川　また、国連事務総長として、あなたは人権に取り組む必要があると思います。

**潘守護霊**　人権？　人権ならいいよ、OK、OK。分かる、分かる、分かる。

石川　ええ。例えば、あなたは、胡錦濤（こきんとう）前国家主席に会った時にも、中国の人権問題について言及（げんきゅう）しませんでした。

**潘守護霊**　中国の人権問題なんて、それは非常に非常に非常に難しい、古典的な問題だろう！　中国には、人権なんて、ないんだ。

**Ishikawa**  Yes. You know very well, so you need to...

**Ban's G.S.**  No, no, nothing in that country!

**Ishikawa**  So you need to resolve this problem, right?

**Ban's G.S.**  Oh, OK. China should follow South Korea. It's a good choice.

**Ishikawa**  So you should talk to President Xi Jinping directly.

**Ban's G.S.**  China is becoming a greater economic power and political power. But there are no such kinds of human rights in China, so they should learn from South Korea about human rights. South Korea can get, at that time, economic power and political power from China. Both of us want to change the

8 韓国と中国が協力して日本の「危険な」政府を変えたい

石川　はい。よくご存じですね。では、あなたは……。


潘守護霊　いやいや、あの国には、何もない！

石川　あなたは、この問題を解決する必要がありますよね。

潘守護霊　ああ、分かった。中国は韓国に倣うべきだ。それがいい選択だ。

石川　ですから、直接、習近平主席と話をされるべきです。


潘守護霊　中国は、経済的にも政治的にも、大国になってきている。しかし、中国には、人権というものがない。だから、韓国から人権について学ぶべきだね。そのとき韓国は、中国から経済力と政治力を手に入れることができる。我々は両国とも、日本人の心や日本の政府を、安倍首相の政策による日本のタカ派で右派の主権を、変え

mind of Japanese people or the Japanese government, the Japanese hawkish, right-wing sovereignty of Prime Minister Abe's policy. It's very dangerous from the eyes of the U.N., so Korean people and the Chinese people must rely on each other and cooperate with each other, and stop the Abe power, Abenomics, in the context of military power. We should stop him.

**Ishikawa**  But I think China's military budget is increasing more rapidly than Japan.

**Ban's G.S.**  It's OK, OK.

**Ishikawa**  About 10 percent every year. So compared with China, it's not a big issue.

**Ban's G.S.**  They are peaceful people, so it's OK. The Japanese are very, very evil people.

**Ishikawa**  Why do you call them peaceful people?

たいわけだ。国連の目から見ると、非常に危険だ。だから、韓国人と中国人はお互いに頼り合って、協力し合って、安倍勢力を、軍事力という意味での「アベノミクス」を食い止めなければならない。彼を止めなければならないわけだよ。

石川　しかし、中国の軍事費は日本よりも急増していると思います。

潘守護霊　それは大丈夫、大丈夫だ。

石川　毎年10％ほど増えています。その中国に比べれば、大した問題ではありません。

潘守護霊　彼らは、平和的な国民だから、いいんだ。日本人は、すごくすごく悪い国民だからね。

石川　なぜ、平和的な国民と呼ぶんですか。あなたは「中

You said in China, there are no human rights, right?

**Ban's G.S.** Japan used to be a very demon-ish country. So, it's quite different. They were intruded by Japan, so they have the right to protect their country.

# 9 Purpose of Promoting Comfort Women Campaign in the U.S.: "Permanent Member South Korea"

**Ishikawa** So, I want to talk about the comfort women issue.

**Ban's G.S.** Comfort women... Bad theme. He (Oikawa) is laughing (audience laughs). No, no.

**Oikawa** This is a good topic.

**Ban's G.S.** I will say nothing. OK?

国には人権がない」とおっしゃいましたよね。

**潘守護霊** 日本は、かつて非常に悪魔的な国だった。だから、まったく違うよ。彼らは日本から侵略されたわけだから、自分たちの国を守る権利がある。

# 9 アメリカでの慰安婦問題推進の目的は「韓国が常任理事国になるため」

**石川** では、慰安婦問題について話をしたいと思います。

**潘守護霊** 慰安婦か。嫌なテーマだなあ。彼（及川氏）は笑ってるよ（会場笑）。いや、いや。

**及川** これはいいテーマです。

**潘守護霊** 何もしゃべらないよ。いいかね。

9 Purpose of Promoting Comfort Women Campaign in the U.S.: "Permanent Member South Korea"

**Oikawa**  It's OK. It's OK. You are a guardian spirit. You are not Mr. Ban, OK?

**Ban's G.S.**  Yes, I'm a guardian spirit. I am not Mr. Ban. I'm just a guardian spirit.

**Oikawa**  You can help us solve this problem. OK?

**Ban's G.S.**  OK, OK. Just an opinion.

**Oikawa**  So, comfort women, in the U.S., as you know, the Korean-Americans decided to build a memorial for comfort women in the local cities.

**Ban's G.S.**  It's OK. No problem, no problem.

**Oikawa**  There must be a strategy or grand plan among the Koreans or some other people. So, if you know about that, please let us know.

## 9　アメリカでの慰安婦問題推進の目的は「韓国が常任理事国になるため」

**及川**　大丈夫です、大丈夫です。あなたは守護霊で、潘氏ではありませんから、大丈夫でしょう？

**潘守護霊**　そうだ、私は守護霊であって、潘氏ではない。ただの守護霊だ。

**及川**　この問題の解決に力を貸していただけますよね。

**潘守護霊**　分かった、分かった。単なる意見だからね。

**及川**　慰安婦ですが、アメリカでは、ご存じの通り、韓国系アメリカ人が、地方都市に慰安婦の記念碑を建てることを決めました。

**潘守護霊**　構わんさ。問題ない、何の問題もない。

**及川**　韓国人か、あるいは他の誰かが、戦略ないし大きな計画を持ってやっているに違いありません。それについてご存じでしたら、ぜひ教えてください。

9 Purpose of Promoting Comfort Women Campaign in the U.S.: "Permanent Member South Korea"

**Ban's G.S.** Hmm. It's OK. If American citizens welcome building up statues of comfort women, it's OK. No problem. They are a country of liberty, so there's no problem. If Japan wants to protest against that, Japanese people should insist on that matter. But even the Japanese newspapers and TV cooperate with this trend to construct the statues of comfort women, so you should fight against your enemy in your own country.

**Oikawa** You're right, you're right. Yes, we have an enemy within.

**Ban's G.S.** Yes.

**Oikawa** OK. So, what is the purpose? What is the ultimate purpose of promoting the comfort women campaign in the U.S.? Why in the U.S.?

**Ban's G.S.** Why in the U.S.? It's because South

## 9 アメリカでの慰安婦問題推進の目的は「韓国が常任理事国になるため」

潘守護霊　うーん。構わない。アメリカ国民が慰安婦像を建てることを歓迎すると言うんなら、構わんだろう。問題ない。アメリカは自由の国だから、問題ない。日本がそれについて抗議したいなら、日本人がその問題に関して主張すべきだ。だけど、日本の新聞やテレビでさえも、この慰安婦像建立の流れに協力してるじゃないか。君たちは、自分たちの国にいる敵と戦うべきだろう。

及川　その通りです。その通りです。ええ、私たちには、内なる敵がいます。

潘守護霊　そうだ。

及川　分かりました。しかし、目的は何でしょうか。アメリカで慰安婦問題を推進する運動の最終目的は何なのでしょうか。なぜ、アメリカなのでしょうか。

潘守護霊　「なぜアメリカなのか」と言えば、韓国が国連

## 9 Purpose of Promoting Comfort Women Campaign in the U.S.: "Permanent Member South Korea"

Korea should be a permanent member of the U.N. I hope. So, we need the support of the citizens of the United States. We, South Korean people, and the people of the U.S. should keep a league, strong league in the near future. And Japan should drop out from this league, from the U.S.-Japan treaty. Japan will, in the near future, abandon this treaty because Okinawa's problem cannot be solved by Prime Minister Abe. So, there will be a civil war in Japan in the near future. I think within these five years. So, Okinawa will ask the citizens to make some kind of vote on which country they should choose, whether they want to become Korean people, Chinese people or Japanese people. There must be such kind of referendum or such kind of voting. I think so. Japan will have a civil war in the near future.

## 9 アメリカでの慰安婦問題推進の目的は「韓国が常任理事国になるため」

の常任理事国になるべきだからだよ。そうなるといいねえ。だから、アメリカ国民からの支持が必要なわけだ。我々韓国人とアメリカ人は同盟を維持するべきだ。近い将来に、強い同盟にするんだ。そして日本は、この同盟から脱落(だつらく)しないといけない。日米条約からね。日本は近い将来、この条約を破棄(はき)するだろう。なぜなら、沖縄(おきなわ)問題は安倍首相では解決できないからね。だから近いうちに、この5年以内に、日本は内戦をすると思うね。沖縄は、どの国を選ぶべきか、韓国人になりたいのか、中国人になりたいのか、日本人になりたいのかを選ぶための、投票のようなことをやるだろうな。そういう住民投票か採決のようなことをやるに違いないと思うね。日本では、近い将来、内戦が起きると思う。

# 10 The U.N. is Not a Fair Institution from its Founding

**Oikawa**  So, it sounds like there's somebody managing a hidden strategy, an international strategy.

**Ban's G.S.**  A hidden international strategy?

**Oikawa**  That's why you became a Korean secretary-general and by using the power of your position…

**Ban's G.S.**  Of course, of course.

**Oikawa**  …are you doing something right?

**Ban's G.S.**  It's the main, main, main, main plan of South Korea, of the South Korean government. And, of course, the president of South Korea and the president of China (laughs). I'm spying.

## １０　国連は設立当初から「公平な機関ではない」

及川　隠れた戦略、国際戦略を操っている人がいそうですね。

潘守護霊　隠れた国際戦略？

及川　だから、あなたが韓国人の事務総長になったわけですが、その地位の力を使って……。

潘守護霊　もちろん、当たり前だろう。

及川　何か正しいことをやっていますか？

潘守護霊　それが韓国の、韓国政府の、メインのメインのメインのメインの計画なんだよ。そしてもちろん、韓国大統領や、中国の国家主席にとっても、だ（笑）。私はスパイ行為をしているんだ。

## 10 The U.N. is Not a Fair Institution from its Founding

**Ishikawa**  Yes, so after you took office in 2007, the number of South Korean staff in the U.N. jumped by 25 percent.

**Ban's G.S.**  Of course. Jumped!

**Ishikawa**  Yes, it increased 25 percent in just one year.

**Ban's G.S.**  We need money from Japan. That's all. No people, no staff from Japan.

**Ishikawa**  Yes, we donated a lot of money.

**Ban's G.S.**  Japanese people cannot speak English, so just money. We need money, more money.

**Ishikawa**  We are the second largest donator, right?

**Ban's G.S.**  Yes, yes, yes.

10　国連は設立当初から「公平な機関ではない」

石川　ええ、あなたが 2007 年に就任してから、国連における韓国人スタッフの数が 25％急増しました。

潘守護霊　もちろんだ。急増！

石川　ええ、たった１年で 25％も、急激に増えました。

潘守護霊　我々は、日本からお金が必要なんだ。それだけで結構。人は要らない。日本からはスタッフは要らない。

石川　ええ、私たちは、多くの額を寄付しました。

潘守護霊　日本人は英語が話せないから、お金だけなのよ。我々にはお金が必要だからさ。もっと金だよ。

石川　私たちは、２番目に大きな拠出国ですよね。

潘守護霊　ああ、そう、そう。

## 10 The U.N. is Not a Fair Institution from its Founding

**Ishikawa**  So you need to hear our opinion, the Japanese opinion.

**Ban's G.S.**  But we don't need any staff from Japan. Japanese people are evil-natured. This is, of course, the opinion of the guardian spirit. Don't think that this is the opinion of Mr. Ban. It's just the guardian spirit's opinion (hits the table several times). Evil-natured.

**Ishikawa**  But your nepotism or your favoritism is criticized severely, not only by Japan, but by the staff of the U.N., too. For example, your Indian son-in-law was appointed to a key role.

**Ban's G.S.**  Hmm… you talk a lot.

**Ishikawa**  Yes, Japanese need to talk a lot.

**Ban's G.S.**  As a Japanese, you should shut up!

石川　ですから、あなたがたは、私たち日本人の意見を聞く必要があります。

潘守護霊　だが、日本からのスタッフは要らない。日本人は性格が悪いからな。もちろん、これは守護霊の意見だよ。潘氏の意見だとは思わないでくれよ。単なる守護霊の意見だ（机を数回たたく）。性格が悪い。

石川　しかし、あなたの身内びいき、えこひいきは、日本からだけでなく、国連のスタッフからも厳しく批判されています。例えば、あなたのインド人の義理の息子が重要な役職に任命されました。

潘守護霊　うーん、君はよくしゃべるねえ。

石川　ええ。日本人は、もっと主張しなければなりません。

潘守護霊　日本人なんだから、黙りなさい！　日本人は、

Japanese people don't speak. They are silent. It's their good point. Be silent, keep silent. It's the good nature of Japanese people.

**Ishikawa**  Yes, actually, Japanese people have a beautiful misunderstanding that the U.N. is a fair, neutral institution.

**Ban's G.S.**  No, no. The U.N. is a league of countries that won in World War II. It's working in the favor of the victorious countries. I mean the U.N. belongs to the anti-fascism countries.

**Ishikawa**  But, the U.N. is not a fair institution. For example, it was founded by…

**Ban's G.S.**  It's not fair, of course! From the beginning it has not been fair. It's not fair. It depends on one category, one favoritism.

しゃべらないもんだ。彼らは無口だ。それが彼らのいいところだ。静かにしろ。静かにしておけ。それが日本人の性格のいいところだ。

石川　ええ。実際、日本人は「国連は公平で中立な機関である」という美しい誤解をしています。


潘守護霊　いやいや。国連は、第二次世界大戦の戦勝国の同盟なんだよ。勝利した国々の便宜のために機能してるんだ。要するに国連は、反ファシズムの国々に属しているわけだ。

石川　しかし、国連は公平な機関ではありません。例えば、設立したのは……。

潘守護霊　公平なんかじゃないよ。当たり前だろう！　最初から公平じゃなかった。公平じゃない。それは、一方のカテゴリー、一方に対する、ひいきによっているんだ。

**Ishikawa**  For example, you had an enemy clause, or…

**Ban's G.S.**  So, anti-Japan, anti-Germany, and anti-Italy; it's the founding opinion of the U.N. The concept of the U.N. started in 1944, before the end of World War II, so please think about this purpose.

**Ishikawa**  Let me make this clear. So, you think that the U.N. is not a fair institution. It's not a fair institution, right?

**Ban's G.S.**  Sometimes, fairness depends on the period or the trend of that age. I mean, the U.N. set free South Korea, so the U.N. is a good organization. But it's not good for Japanese people from the beginning. Sorry, but it's not fair for Japan, for Germany, or for other fascist countries.

## 10　国連は設立当初から「公平な機関ではない」

石川　例えば、敵国条項があったり……。


潘守護霊　だから、反日、反ドイツ、反イタリアなわけだ。それが国連発足当時の意見なんだよ。国連の概念が始まったのが1944年で、第二次世界大戦が終わる前だったんだから、その目的を考えてくれよ。

石川　はっきりさせてください。あなたは、国連は公平な機関ではないとお考えなんですね。公平な機関ではないと？

潘守護霊　時には、公平さというのは、時期やその時代の流れにもよるんだ。つまり、国連は韓国を解放したから、いい組織なんだけど、日本人にとっては、最初から、いいものじゃなかったのさ。申し訳ないけどね。でも、国連は日本に対して公平ではないし、ドイツに対しても、他のファシズム国家に対しても公平ではないわけよ。

**Ishikawa**  Yes, Japanese people need to know that fact. Thank you so much.

**Ban's G.S.**  Yes. It's not fair. It depends on western opinion.

# 11 We Cannot Criticize America, the Owner of the U.N.

**Ichikawa**  Among the permanent members of the U.N. Security Council, there are socialist countries like Russia and atheist countries like China. So, I would like to ask about your opinions on Russia and China. First, could I ask you about that?

**Ban's G.S.**  At first, they were not socialist countries. That's the problem. At first, they were not, but now, or after the world war, they became socialist. That will make another cold war and it might become the cause of the Third World War. So the U.N. is a

石川　ええ、日本人は、その事実を知る必要がありますね。ありがとうございます。

潘守護霊　うん。公平なんかじゃないよ。西洋の考えによっているんだ。

## １１　国連のオーナーであるアメリカのことは批判できない

市川　国連安全保障理事会の常任理事国の中には、ロシアのような社会主義国や中国のような無神論国家もあります。そこで、ロシアや中国に対するあなたのお考えを伺いたいのですが、まず、伺ってもよろしいでしょうか。

潘守護霊　彼らは最初は、社会主義国家じゃなかったのよ。それが問題なんだ。最初は違ったけど、今は、つまり大戦後、社会主義になったんだ。それが次の冷戦を生み、さらには第三次世界大戦の火種になるかもしれない。だから国連は、均衡を保つ役割なんだ。国連が彼らの均衡

balancer. I think the U.N. is a balancer for them.

**Ishikawa**  So I would like to ask about the future of the U.N. For example, should the U.N. have its own permanent standing army?

**Ban's G.S.**  Hmm…

**Ishikawa**  I think you said that the U.N. had no power, right?

**Ban's G.S.**  But it's difficult. For example, the Russian troop and the American troop should make a conflict in the Syrian area, but the U.N. army cannot work at that time, so it's very difficult. If all the members of the Security Council agree to conduct some military action, it will be effective. But after the cold war, I think it's very difficult.

**Ishikawa**  Yes, and additionally, the fiscal cliff.

を保つんだと思うね。

石川　では、国連の未来について、お伺いしたいと思います。例えば、国連は、独自の常備軍を持つべきでしょうか。

潘守護霊　うーん……。

石川　あなたは、「国連は無力だ」とおっしゃいましたよね。

潘守護霊　でも、それは難しいね。例えば、ロシア軍とアメリカ軍がシリア地域で対立するはずだ。そうなれば、国連軍は機能しない。だから非常に難しい。安保理のすべての国が、軍事行動を起こすことに賛成すれば効果はあるだろうけれども、冷戦後は、それは非常に難しいと思う。

石川　そうですね。さらには、財政の崖（がけ）があります。ア

## 11 We Cannot Criticize America, the Owner of the U.N.

America has a financial problem, right?

**Ban's G.S.** Ah, financial problem again. Oh.

**Ishikawa** I think that maybe Obama has little diplomatic skills.

**Ban's G.S.** Top secret. The U.N. is… (laughs) Do you know where the U.N. headquarters is? You know? You know?

**Ishikawa** In New York, right?

**Ban's G.S.** Yes, yes, New York. New York, but it's not the U.S.A. The U.N. is one spot, like the Vatican. It's not America, but it's in America. We are like the Vatican, or like Israel surrounded by Arabic countries. So, we can say anything except to be aggressive to the United States. It's very difficult to condemn America because they are the owner of the tenant (laughs).

メリカには財政問題がありますよね。

**潘守護霊** ああ、また財政問題か。おお。

**石川** オバマは、あまり外交手腕に長けていないのではないかと思います。

**潘守護霊** 最高機密だ。国連は……（笑）。国連本部がどこにあるか知ってる？　知ってる？　知ってる？

**石川** ニューヨークですよね。

**潘守護霊** そう、そう、ニューヨークだ。ニューヨークだけど、アメリカじゃない。国連はバチカンみたいな、一つの点にすぎない。アメリカじゃないけど、アメリカの中にあるわけだ。バチカンみたいな、あるいは、アラブ諸国に囲まれているイスラエルみたいなものだ。だから、我々は何を言ってもいいけれど、アメリカ合衆国に対して攻撃的なことだけは駄目だ。アメリカを非難する

## 11 We Cannot Criticize America, the Owner of the U.N.

**Ishikawa**  So, you can't say anything to the superpowers such as the U.S.A. or China?

**Ban's G.S.**  South Korea can do nothing to them.

**Ishikawa**  For example, Former Secretary-General Annan or other predecessors said what they think. But you do not say anything. That's why you are criticized for being too bureaucratic or incompetent.

**Ban's G.S.**  But America, the United States, can do something about that. Because if Secretary-General Annan says something against the U.S. policy, they can slash the U.S. budget set aside for the U.N. So, it's a problem. They are the owner of the U.N.

のは、非常に難しい。彼らがテナントのオーナーだからね（笑）。

石川　では、あなたは、アメリカや中国などの大国に対して何も言えないのですか。

潘守護霊　韓国は、彼らに対して何もできない。

石川　例えば、アナン前事務総長や他の前任者たちは、自分の考えを発言していました。しかし、あなたは何もおっしゃいません。だから、あなたは、あまりにも官僚的であるとか無能であると批判されているわけです。

潘守護霊　しかし、アメリカは、アメリカ合衆国は、そういう場合に、何かやれてしまうわけだ。なぜなら、もしアナン事務総長が何かアメリカの政策に反することを言ったら、アメリカは国連向けの予算を削減することができる。これは問題なんだ。彼らが国連のオーナーなんだよ。

# 12 Guardian Spirit: "I Have No Leadership"

**Oikawa**  OK, so the current situation in the Middle East. You held a U.N. general assembly and many world leaders got together, right? And, this year, the new Iranian president, Rouhani became very popular.

**Ban's G.S.**  Iranian President! Ah, Rouhani.

**Oikawa**  And he still insists that they don't have any nuclear weapons, that they are not developing any nuclear weapons, and that they are just developing nuclear power for peaceful purposes. But if you know anything about this, please let us know.

**Ban's G.S.**  Ah… You are very smart, very smart, of course. You should change, and take the risk in place of the U.N. You can, of course. Please say something to the Iranian president or the Israeli president and

## １２　私にはリーダーシップなんかない

及川　では、中東の現状ですが、国連総会があって、世界の指導者が大勢集まりましたね。今年になって、イランの新しい大統領、ロウハニが、非常に人気を得ています。

潘守護霊　イラン大統領！　ああ、ロウハニね。

及川　そして彼は、いまだに、「自分たちは核兵器を持っていないし開発もしていない。ただ、平和的目的のために核エネルギーを開発しているだけだ」と主張しています。しかし、もしこれについて何かご存じでしたら、ぜひ教えていただけますでしょうか。

潘守護霊　ああ……君は非常に頭がいいね、頭がいい、当然だ。君が変わって、国連の代わりにリスクを取るべきだ。当然、君ならできるよ。イランの大統領やイスラエルの大統領に対して物を言って、彼らと戦ってくださ

fight against them. It's OK, no problem.

**Oikawa**  I just want to ask you if you know whether the Iranian government is still developing nuclear weapons or not.

**Ban's G.S.**  I know, I know, I know, I know. But we can do nothing about that. It depends. It's almost the same as the Syrian problem. It depends on which conclusion Russia, China and America choose. We can do nothing.

**Ichikawa**  It depends on your leadership.

**Ban's G.S.**  No, I have no leadership (audience laughs).

**Oikawa**  OK, so Iran has nuclear weapons, and they are just about to finish developing nuclear weapons. Is this true or not?

いよ。いいよ、問題ない。

及川　私は、イラン政府がまだ核兵器を開発しているかどうかについて、あなたがご存じかどうか、お聞きしたいだけなのです。

潘守護霊　知ってる、知ってる、知ってる、知ってる。でも、それに関しては何もできないね。場合によるな。シリア問題とほとんど同じことだ。ロシアや中国やアメリカが、どういった結論を選ぶかにかかっている。我々には何もできない。

市川　あなたのリーダーシップにかかっているんです。

潘守護霊　いや、私にはリーダーシップなんかないもん（会場笑）。

及川　分かりました。つまり、イランは核兵器を持っていて、今まさに核兵器を完成させるところだということですね。そうですか、違いますか。

## 12 Guardian Spirit: "I Have No Leadership"

**Ban's G.S.**  Hmm… ah… Their hidden intention must be to create nuclear weapons. I guess so.

**Oikawa**  Despite the statement of Iran's new president Rouhani?

**Ban's G.S.**  Of course the Islamic people can lie. Muhammad, the founder of that religion, said a lot of lies. So, they are liars by nature. So, almost everything from them should be thought of as a lie. So the president of Israel never believes what they say. President Rouhani is a very, very wise man. He is also a difficult person, like Japanese people.

**Oikawa**  Why is he difficult?

**Ban's G.S.**  Because Mr. Rouhani can use, as Japanese people say, "*Honne* and *Tatemae*." His real meaning and formal saying are quite different. That's the problem. We cannot rely on what he says.

## 12　私にはリーダーシップなんかない

**潘守護霊**　うーん……んー……彼らの秘めたる意図は、核兵器を作ることに違いない。そう思うよ。

**及川**　イランの新しい大統領、ロウハニの声明にもかかわらず？

**潘守護霊**　もちろん、イスラム教徒は嘘がつけるからさ。開祖のムハンマドがたくさん嘘をついたからね。だから、彼らは生まれつき、嘘つきなのよ。彼らから出てくるものは、ほぼ全部、嘘だと思わないといかん。だからイスラエルの大統領は、彼らの言うことは決して信じない。ロウハニ大統領は、実に実に賢い男だ。そして、難しい人間でもある。日本人みたいにね。

**及川**　なぜ難しいのですか。

**潘守護霊**　ロウハニさんは、日本人が言うところの「本音と建て前」が使える人なんだよ。本当の考えと公式的な言葉は、まったく違ってるんだ。そこが問題だね。彼の言うことは信用できない。

**Oikawa**  However, he used very positive words and is full of smiles, so the international community is accepting him.

**Ban's G.S.**  (laughs)

**Oikawa**  But that is a lie, right?

**Ban's G.S.**  I don't believe him. I don't believe him. He is evil indeed.

**Oikawa**  Thank you very much.

**Ban's G.S.**  Mm.

**Oikawa**  That's good information.

**Ban's G.S.**  Is it OK? It's an opinion of the spirit. Not the opinion of Mr. Ban.

**及川** ですが、彼は非常に前向きな言葉を使っていましたし、満面の笑顔を見せていますから、国際社会は彼を受け入れていますよ。

**潘守護霊** （笑）。

**及川** でも、それは嘘なんですね？

**潘守護霊** 私は彼を信じないね。信じない。本当に悪い奴だよ。

**及川** ありがとうございました。

**潘守護霊** うん。

**及川** いい情報でした。

**潘守護霊** よかったのかな？　霊の意見だからね。潘氏の意見じゃないよ。

# 13 Secretary-General is "Secret General"

**Oikawa**  OK. This is a similar issue, but the Syrian issue is now, almost depends on what Russia and U.S. agree as the way to deal with that. Also, Assad is forgiven. He's also accepted by the global community because he has chemical weapons but never used them against his own people. But I think you know about that.

**Ban's G.S.**  Ha, ha, ha, ha, ha, ha.

**Oikawa**  So you know the truth, right?

**Ban's G.S.**  Of course, of course, of course, of course, of course. But, but, but, but, but… I'm the secretary-general. A secretary-general is a "secret general" (audience laughs). You know?

## １３　事務総長とは「秘密総長」である

及川　はい。これも似たような問題ですが、シリア問題は今、ほぼ、ロシアとアメリカがどういった対処法で合意するかにかかっています。アサドも許されました。彼も国際社会に受け入れられてしまいました。「化学兵器を所有してはいるけれども、自国民に対して化学兵器を使ってはいない」ということで。しかし、それについてご存じだと思います。

潘守護霊　ハッハッハッハッハッハ。

及川　では、真相をご存じなんですね。

潘守護霊　当然、当然、当然、当然、当然。だが、だが、だが、だが、だが……。私は事務総長なんだよ。事務総長（secretary-general）というのは「秘密総長」（secret general）なのよ（会場笑）。分かるかな？

**Oikawa**  I know. But you are the guardian spirit. You are not himself.

**Ban's G.S.**  Ah, it's a problem of the quality of the president. The quality problem of President Putin and President Obama. The quality of Obama is, blablablabla… I can't say exactly, but it's sinking deep into the sea. But President Putin, he can do *yawara*, *judo*. He is very skillful in his presidency. He's a powerful and skillful politician. So Mr. Obama cannot resist his power, I guess. But I'm a "secret general" so I can't say any more.

**Ishikawa**  I think you were once a foreign minister of South Korea. Recently, North Korea restarted the nuclear reactor. So what do you think of the Six-Party Talks or the nuclear issue of North Korea?

**Ban's G.S.**  Difficult questions only.

及川　分かります。でも、あなたは守護霊であって、本人ではありません。

潘守護霊　ああ、それはね、大統領の資質の問題なのよ。プーチン大統領とオバマ大統領の資質の問題。オバマの資質は、なんたらかんたら……。正確には言えないけど、海の底深く沈んでいこうとしているね。でもプーチン大統領は、「柔」「柔道」をやるからな。彼は大統領としての技能が非常に高い。政治家として力量があるし、腕もいい。だからオバマさんは、彼のパワーに抵抗できないと思うね。でも、私は「秘密総長」だから、それ以上は言えないな。

石川　あなたは以前、韓国の外務大臣でした。最近、北朝鮮は原子炉を再スタートさせました。そこで、６カ国協議や北朝鮮の核問題については、どうお考えですか。

潘守護霊　難しい質問しかしないなあ。

**Ishikawa**  Is it a good thing for South Korean people that North Korea, who are the same race as them, has nuclear weapons?

**Ban's G.S.**  Hmm… President Park is approaching the president of China for that reason. If she can succeed in keeping good friendship with the Chinese leader, China can, of course, check and protect them against the expansion of North Korea. This means the security of South Korea. That is the dynamics of politics. So the South Korean leader wants to use the U.N. power, of course, and is also depending on the secretary-general. But in the end, she will ask the Chinese president to stop North Korea. That's all. In this context, there is no problem of Japan. Mr. Abe should do nothing because it's complicated. It will be complicated so he should do nothing.

石川　韓国の人たちにとっては、同じ民族の北朝鮮が核兵器を持つのはいいことなのでしょうか。

潘守護霊　うーん……。朴大統領が中国の国家主席に接近しているのも、それが理由なわけだよ。彼女は中国の指導者と友好関係を保つことに成功すれば、中国は当然、チェックして、北朝鮮の拡張から守れるからね。それは韓国の安全を意味するわけだ。それが政治の力学だな。だから韓国の指導者は、当然、国連の力も利用したいし、事務総長のことも頼っている。でも最終的には彼女は、中国の国家主席に「北朝鮮を止めてほしい」と頼むだろうね。それだけのことだよ。この状況においては、日本は問題ない。安倍さんは何もすべきではないね。複雑だから。複雑になるだろうから、彼は何もすべきではない。

# 14 Comparing the Figures: People Kidnapped vs. Possible Casualties of a War Between North and South Korea

**Ishikawa**  Speaking of North Korea, not only Japanese people but South Korean people were abducted and kidnapped by North Korea, right? So…

**Ban's G.S.**  (clicks tongue) Kidnapping and human trafficking… ah, this is a problem. It's a problem, but the evidence is not so confirmed. If there would occur another war between North and South Korea, there will be tens of thousands of casualties in that war. If we think about that, the number of those who were kidnapped are very small. So, it's very difficult. From Japan, it might be about one hundred or so, or maybe a little more. From South Korea, several hundred people have been kidnapped by the North. There might be people who are still alive but some of them might be already dead. If this causes another

# １４　拉致人数と、南北朝鮮で戦争が起きた場合の死者数を比較

石川　北朝鮮について言えば、日本人だけでなく韓国人も、北朝鮮によって拉致、誘拐されていますよね。ですから……。

**潘守護霊**　（舌打ち）誘拐に人身売買……。ああ、それは問題だ。問題だが、証拠がそれほど固まっていないのよ。もし南北朝鮮の間でまた戦争が起こったら、何十万人も戦死者が出ることになるだろう。そのことを考えた場合、誘拐に遭った人数は非常に少ない。だから、非常に難しいんだよ。日本からは、百人ぐらいか、もう少し多かったかな。韓国からは何百人も北に誘拐されている。その人たちの中には生きている人もいれば、もう亡くなっている人もいるだろうけれど、そのことでまた戦争が起きたら、近い将来に何十万も人が死ぬことになる。だから、そこのところを深く考えないといけないわけだ。

war, it means tens of thousands of people will die in the near future. So we have to think deep about that.

**Oikawa**  But you are a part of Korean people. There are many families and parents who lost their children because they were kidnapped by the other half of your country.

**Ban's G.S.**  I know, I know.

**Oikawa**  So you must have a mind of love and mercy, right?

**Ban's G.S.**  Love and mercy…

**Oikawa**  And you have power so there must be something you can do, something you can give more effort into doing or room for more effort on what you can do. Do you have any determination on doing something to solve this problem?

## 14　拉致人数と、南北朝鮮で戦争が起きた場合の死者数を比較

及川　しかし、あなたは韓国人の一人であって、自分の国のもう片方によって子供を誘拐されて失っている家族や親がたくさんいるわけですよ。

潘守護霊　分かってる、分かってる。

及川　ですから、あなたにも愛の心や慈悲の心がおありでしょう？

潘守護霊　愛や慈悲か……。

及川　しかも権力をお持ちなわけですから、何かあなたにできることが、もっとやろうと努力することが、自分のできることに関してもっと努力の余地が、あるはずです。この問題を解決するために、何かをする決意はおありですか。

14 Comparing the Figures: People Kidnapped vs. Possible Casualties of a War Between North and South Korea

**Ban's G.S.** If we are to be determined to save such kidnapped people, we will ask the United States, the Seventh Fleet. Then the navy will attack North Korea and occupy Pyongyang. At that time, maybe a lot of people will die so it's a very difficult matter.

**Oikawa** However, you can speak the Korean language. You can talk to the people in North Korea. Why don't you go to Pyongyang yourself?

**Ban's G.S.** Ah, I don't want to die.

(Audience laughs)

**Oikawa** OK, thank you.

**Ishikawa** You lack leadership.

**Ban's G.S.** Ah, no, no, no. I'm wise. That's all.

14　拉致人数と、南北朝鮮で戦争が起きた場合の死者数を比較

**潘守護霊**　そういう誘拐された人たちを救おうと決意するなら、アメリカに、第七艦隊(だいななかんたい)に頼むよ。そうすれば海軍が北朝鮮を攻撃して、ピョンヤンを占領する。そうなれば、死者がたくさん出るだろうね。だから非常に難しい問題なんだ。

**及川**　しかし、あなたは韓国語が話せるじゃないですか。北朝鮮の国民に話しかけることができるじゃないですか。なぜ自分でピョンヤンに行かないのですか。

**潘守護霊**　ああ、死にたくないからね。

（会場笑）

**及川**　ああ、ありがとうございました。

**石川**　あなたにはリーダーシップが欠けています。

**潘守護霊**　ああ、違う違う違う。賢明(けんめい)なんだよ。それだけ。

**Ichikawa** But what you are thinking about is very…

**Ban's G.S.** They are not sane. We cannot expect a common, reasonable conversation. We cannot expect. They are crazy. In my mind, they are crazy and are not common people. Their common sense is quite different from the global sense worldwide. So we just pray for the end of North Korea.

# 15 I am an Adjuster Who Just Thinks About the Benefit of South Korea

**Oikawa** But I have a great idea. You are criticized a lot by people, right? But if you make a surprise visit to North Korea and try to solve this problem, people in the world will admire you.

**Ban's G.S.** No, no, no. I have no such kind of desire. I'm a Buddhist. I'm a Buddhist and I also

市川　しかし、あなたの考えは非常に……。

潘守護霊　彼らは正気じゃないからさ。普通の、道理にかなった話し合いなんか望めないんだよ。望めない。彼らは狂ってる。私が思うに、彼らは狂っていて普通の人間じゃない。彼らの常識は、世界規模のグローバルな感覚とはまったく違うんだ。だから、北朝鮮が終わることを祈るしかない。

## １５　私は韓国の利益だけを考えている「調整者」

及川　ですが、名案があります。あなたは人々から批判されてばかりですよね。でも、もしあなたが北朝鮮を電撃訪問して、この問題を解決しようとすれば、世界中の人々があなたを称賛しますよ。

潘守護霊　いや、いや、いや。私には、そんな欲はないよ。私は仏教徒だからさ。仏教徒だしキリスト教も大好きだ

love Christianity so I have no such kind of, or I'm not seeking for such kind of fame or worldly desire. I'm aiming to become a Buddhist saint, so I think of doing nothing.

**Oikawa**  That's a great idea, but what is your mission? What is your personal goal as the secretary-general?

**Ban's G.S.**  Personal goal? Personal goal is... my position now is the goal.

**Ishikawa**  (laughs)

**Ban's G.S.**  Being the secretary-general. That is the goal of Korean people. I am the star of the Korean people.

**Ishikawa**  What do you mean?

から、その手の、その手の名声やこの世的な欲なんか求めてないんだ。仏教の聖者になることを目指してるんで、何もしようとは思わない。

及川　それは素晴らしい考えですが、でも、あなたの使命は何なんですか。事務総長としての、あなたの個人的なゴールは何ですか。

**潘守護霊**　個人的なゴール？　個人的なゴールなら……今の地位がゴールだよ。

石川　（笑）

**潘守護霊**　事務総長であること。それが韓国人にとってのゴールだよ。私は韓国人のスターなのよ。

石川　どういう意味でしょうか。

## 15 I am an Adjuster Who Just Thinks About the Benefit of South Korea

**Ban's G.S.**  I am the "purpose" of the clever Korean people.

**Ichikawa**  So does it mean that you are just thinking about the benefit of South Korea?

**Ban's G.S.**  Yeah, of course. Ah, no, no, no, no, no, no, no, no!

**Ichikawa**  "Of course"? You said "of course," right?

**Ban's G.S.**  Yes. Yeah, yeah, yeah. Just a moment, just a moment, just a moment. I just wanted to say that I am the hope of the Korean young people. Hm, hm, hm.

**Ishikawa**  So for you, South Korean interests are the most important?

**Ban's G.S.**  Ah, no, no, I don't make decisions. I

**潘守護霊** 私は、韓国の優秀な人たちの"目標"なんだよ。

**市川** ということは、あなたは韓国の利益だけを考えているということでしょうか。

**潘守護霊** ああ、当然じゃないか。ああ、違う、違う、違う、違う、違う、違う、違う、違う！

**市川** 当然？「当然」と言われましたね。

**潘守護霊** そうだ。そう、そう、そう。ちょっと待った、ちょっと待った、ちょっと待った。私はただ、私が韓国の若者にとっての希望だということを言いたかっただけなのよ。うん、うん、うん。

**石川** ということは、あなたには韓国の利益が、いちばん大事だということですね。

**潘守護霊** ああ、違う、違う。私は意思決定はしないから。

am not a decision-maker. I am just adjusting. I am an adjuster. I am an adjusting person, so I will do some profit for the peace of the world.

# 16 Japanese People Should Think About Their Sin or Their Fathers' Sin

**Ishikawa**  Then, I have another question. Now, some South Korean people or a court of justice in South Korea are demanding compensation to Japanese companies…

**Ban's G.S.**  (sighs)

**Ishikawa**  Mitsubishi Heavy Industries and Nippon Steel. But according to the agreement between Japan and South Korea in 1965, as you know, "The problems concerning property…"

私は意思決定者じゃなくて、調整してるだけだ。私は調整者なんだよ。調整をする人間なんだ。だから、世界の平和に資するわけだ。

## １６　日本人は自分たちや父祖の罪を考えよ

石川　では、別の質問をさせていただきます。現在、ある韓国人たち、あるいは韓国の裁判所は、日本の企業……。

潘守護霊　（ため息）

石川　三菱重工や新日鉄に賠償請求をしていますね。しかし、1965年に締結された日本と韓国の合意によれば、ご存じのように、「両当事者の財産、」……。

**Ban's G.S.**  New York, New York, New York is busy, busy.

**Ishikawa**  "...rights and interests of the two contracting parties..."

**Ban's G.S.**  (covers ears)

**Ishikawa**  Can you hear me?

**Ban's G.S.**  Oh… ah… hmm…

**Ishikawa**  "have been settled completely and finally." But this is a big problem, right?

**Ban's G.S.**  No, no, no. Small, small, small, minor, minor, minor problem right? OK?

**Ishikawa**  What do you think…

潘守護霊　ニューヨーク、ニューヨーク、ニューヨークは忙しい、忙しいなあ。

石川　「権利、権益などに関する問題は」……。

潘守護霊　（両耳を塞ぐ）

石川　聞こえてますか？

潘守護霊　おお……ああ……うーん……。

石川　「完全かつ最終的に解決した」ということです。ところが、それが大きな問題になっていますね。

潘守護霊　いやいやいや。小さな小さな小さな、マイナーなマイナーなマイナーなマイナーな問題だろう？　分かる？

石川　あなたはどう考えて……。

**Ban's G.S.**  You think too much about that.

**Ishikawa**  ...as the secretary-general of the U.N.?

**Ban's G.S.**  Forget, forget! Forget it!

**Ishikawa**  Please say something.

**Ban's G.S.**  Forgetting is forgiving! I'm the peacemaker! Please forget small, small things. Japan has money. Japan has a lot of money and from what Korean people see...

**Ishikawa**  Now you have good, strong companies like Samsung or Hyundai.

**Ban's G.S.**  Yeah, Samsung and Hyundai. They are exceptions. They are exceptions. Japan has a lot of money so you should think about your sin or your fathers' sin. Your fathers' sin. OK?

潘守護霊　君は、それについて考えすぎなんだよ。

石川　国連の事務総長として。

潘守護霊　忘れて、忘れて！　忘れなさい！

石川　何かおっしゃってください。

潘守護霊　忘れることが、許すことである！　私は調停者なんだから！　頼むから、小さな小さなことは忘れてくれよ。日本はお金があるんだからさ。日本はお金がいっぱいあるんだから、韓国人が考えることは……。

石川　今では韓国にも、優良な、力のある企業がありますよね。サムスンとかヒュンダイとか。

潘守護霊　そう、サムスン、ヒュンダイ。彼らは例外だよ。例外なのよ。日本はお金がいっぱいあるんだから、自分たちの罪とか父祖の罪のことを考えないといけないのよ。父祖の罪。分かる？

# 17 The Tie Between Ban and the Unification Church

**Ishikawa**  Oh, OK. I have another question. Do you have ties with the Unification Church? You said you were Buddhist or Christian.

**Ban's G.S.**  Ah, my family is Buddhist. So that's not Buddhist…

**Ishikawa**  According to the teaching of that religion (Unification Church), Japan is a very bad country.

**Ban's G.S.**  Yeah, it's a religion of South Korean origin, I know.

**Ishikawa**  So does this influence your thought?

**Ban's G.S.**  Its profit is in tune with South Korea. They are insisting that Japan is a bad country, the

# １７　潘氏と統一協会の関係について

石川　はい、はい。もう一つ質問があります。あなたは、統一協会とつながりがありますか？　自分は仏教徒だとかキリスト教徒だとか言われましたが。

**潘守護霊**　ああ、私の一族は仏教徒だよ。だから、それは仏教徒ではない……。

石川　その宗教（統一協会）の教えによると、日本はとても悪い国だそうです。

**潘守護霊**　そうだ、韓国が起源の宗教だな。知ってるよ。

石川　では、それがあなたの考え方に影響していますか。

**潘守護霊**　そこは韓国と利益が一致するんだ。彼らは、「日本は悪い国、エヴァの国で、韓国はアダムの国だ」と言っ

## 17 The Tie Between Ban and the Unification Church

country of Eva, and South Korea is the country of Adam. Adam was deceived by Eva, or Eve. This is the original sin. So Japan should pay money regarding this original sin. This is their issuing point and it's the national profit of South Korea, indeed. The South Korean government just wants to use this point only. And this religious group also has influence on North Korea, so we just want to use this power, the religious power. This benefits South Korea. That's all. I'm a Buddhist, originally. Hmm.

**Ichikawa** Among the secretary-generals until now, you were the only person who didn't disclose his beliefs. I want to confirm: are you a Buddhist?

**Ban's G.S.** Hmm, originally.

**Ichikawa** Originally. How about now? Now? You are a member of...

てるんだよ。アダムはエヴァに、イブにそそのかされた。これが原罪だ。だから日本は、この原罪に関して、金を払わなきゃならん。これが彼らの主張している点で、まさに韓国の国益にもなる。韓国政府は、この点だけ利用したいわけよ。それと、この宗教団体は北朝鮮にも影響力があるから、その力、宗教の力を利用したいだけなんだ。それが韓国の利益になるわけだ。それだけの話だね。私はもともと仏教徒だからさ、うん。

市川　あなたは、今までの事務総長のなかで唯一、ご自身の信仰を開示しませんでした。確認させていただきたいのですが、あなたは仏教徒なのですか。

潘守護霊　うん、もともとはね。

市川　もともとは。今はどうなのでしょうか？　今は？　あなたは会員……。

## 17 The Tie Between Ban and the Unification Church

**Ban's G.S.**  I studied English a lot, so at that time, I learned a lot from the Christian churches. So some part of my spirituality is based on Christianity. I'm originally a Buddhist but some part of my mentality includes Christian-like thinking. So, I'm the worldwide peacemaker. So, I'm like the Buddha and Jesus Christ, or someone next to them, I think. Or, maybe like Gandhi of India.

**Ichikawa**  Then I want to confirm: were you baptized?

**Ban's G.S.**  Oh... I'm a spirit so I don't know exactly. Hmm... I'm a "secret general" so (laughs) it's a difficult question. It's a personal question. I'm a public figure, so please ask me about public problems only.

**Ishikawa**  I have heard a story, where you said yourself, that you bemoaned over your difficulty in

**潘守護霊**　私は英語をよく勉強したから、その当時、キリスト教の教会から学んだことがたくさんあった。だから、私の精神面には、キリスト教がもとになっている部分がある。もとは仏教徒なんだけど、メンタリティの一部にキリスト教的な考え方が入ってる。だから、私は世界的な調停者であるわけよ。だから、仏陀やイエス・キリストみたいな、もしくは彼らに近い人間だと思うなあ。あるいはインドのガンジーみたいな。

**市川**　では、確認させていただきたいのですが、あなたは洗礼をお受けになりましたか。

**潘守護霊**　ああ……私は霊だから、よく分からんけど。うーん……私は「秘密総長」だから（笑）、それは難しい質問だなあ。個人的な質問だ。私は公人だから、公的な問題についてだけ聞いてもらえませんかね。

**石川**　あなたご自身がおっしゃった、次のような話を聞いたことがあります。あなたは困難を、さまざまな問題

overcoming various kinds of problems and you tried to lead by example, but nobody followed. Is this a true story? If so, it means that many people criticized you because you lacked leadership and it means that you are incompetent. That's why nobody followed you.

**Ban's G.S.**  Hmm. Is there any good news about me?

**Ishikawa**  Depends on your (laughs) comments.

**Ban's G.S.**  You are a bad journalist. Japanese!

**Ishikawa**  A fair journalist.

**Ban's G.S.**  Hmm…

を克服できなくて嘆き、範を示して導こうとしたのに、誰もついてこなかったと。これは本当の話ですか？　だとすれば、あなたにはリーダーシップが欠けていたために多くの人から批判されたのであり、無能であることになります。だから、誰もついてこなかったと。


潘守護霊　うーん。私に関して、何かいいニュースはないの？

石川　あなたが（笑）何をおっしゃるかによるでしょう。

潘守護霊　君は、悪いジャーナリストだな。日本人め！

石川　公正なジャーナリストです。

潘守護霊　うーん。

# 18 I'm Not a Leader Who Makes Decisions

**Oikawa**  OK, OK. I have an article with me. This is not a Japanese one. This is a New York Times article. I think you must be checking out all articles on you. This article says, "Where are you Ban Ki-moon?"

**Ban's G.S.**  "Where"?

**Oikawa**  The author said that you are like an invisible secretary-general.

**Ban's G.S.**  "Invisible"?

**Oikawa**  And you are anonymous. That's why, before your term terminates in, is it 2016, U.N. members should get another person. I don't know, but what do you think about this kind of comment or criticism

# １８　私は意思決定をするリーダーではない

及川　分かりました、分かりました。私の手許に一本の記事があります。日本のではなく、ニューヨーク・タイムズの記事です。あなたは、ご自分に関する記事は全部チェックしているはずだと思いますが、この記事には、「潘基文よ、あなたは、どこに？」と書かれています。

潘守護霊　「どこに」？

及川　記者によると、あなたは「目に見えない事務総長」のようなものだそうです。

潘守護霊　「目に見えない」？

及川　また、あなたは自分の名前を出さないそうです。そのため、あなたの任期が満了する 2016 年でしたか、それより前に、国連加盟国は別の人物を探さないといけないそうです。私には分かりませんが、ご自分についての

towards you?

**Ban's G.S.**  Criticizing is their job so it's OK. But I have a more sacred job. Yeah, this is a sacred task. So I must disregard such kind of comments.

**Oikawa**  I understand that you have a sacred job, such as?

**Ban's G.S.**  Such as? Oh, adjusting for world peace.

**Oikawa**  For example?

**Ban's G.S.**  Conflicts.

**Oikawa**  What kind of conflicts?

**Ban's G.S.**  Syrian problem, Korean problem.

## 18　私は意思決定をするリーダーではない

この種のコメントや批判についてはどう思われますか。

潘守護霊　批判するのが彼らの仕事だから、別にいいよ。でも、私にはもっと聖なる仕事があるんだからさ。そう、これは聖なる仕事なのよ。だから、そんなコメントは無視するに限るね。

及川　聖なる仕事があるというのは分かりますが、例えば、どのような？

潘守護霊　例えば？　ああ、世界平和のために調整に当たるとか。

及川　具体的には？

潘守護霊　紛争とか。

及川　どういった紛争でしょうか。

潘守護霊　シリア問題とか、朝鮮問題とか。

## 18 I'm Not a Leader Who Makes Decisions

**Oikawa**  How are you going to help?

**Ban's G.S.**  Japanese problem, Senkaku problem or Dokdo problem. And now is the American economic problem and financial problem, I mean the budget problem. Under such kind of circumstances, how can we act correctly in the world? This is a very difficult problem. America is a great ship that is sinking, so we are in great difficulties. New leader of the world is unknown. I'm not a leader who makes the decision. I'm just the person of adjustment so it's very difficult for me. Maybe I can recommend you to become the secretary-general.

## 18　私は意思決定をするリーダーではない

及川　どのように力を貸すのでしょうか。

潘守護霊　日本の問題、尖閣問題や独島問題、あと、今はアメリカの経済問題や財政問題、つまり予算問題だな。こんな状況のなかで、世界の中でどうすれば正しい行動がとれるのか。非常に難しい問題だ。アメリカは沈みゆく巨大な船だから、我々はきわめて困難な状況に置かれている。誰が世界の新しいリーダーなのか分からない。私は意思決定をするリーダーではない。調整型の人間にすぎないから、私には非常に難しいんだよ。君を事務総長に推薦してもいいかもしれないなあ。

# 19 Mr. Abe Should Destroy Yasukuni Shrine

**Oikawa**  We all understand that it is a very difficult time and that your job is very difficult. However, this is not by chance that you, a Korean, became the secretary-general at this time. There must be a reason. What's your hidden mission? Let us know.

**Ban's G.S.**  Hmm… hidden mission (laughs)? There is no hidden mission. My mission is very clear. My mission is to stop the future danger of Japan. Mr. Abe said, "Japan is back." What does this mean? Japan is back? I know *Superman Returns*. This title, I know.

**Ishikawa**  This means that Japan will become the new world leader.

**Ban's G.S.**  Japan wants to get strong military forces

# １９　安倍氏は靖国神社を壊すべき

及川　今は大変困難な時代で、あなたの仕事が大変難しいことは、私たち全員、理解しています。しかし、この時にあって、韓国人であるあなたが事務総長になられたのは、たまたまではなく、きっと理由があるはずです。あなたの秘密の使命は何なのか、お教えください。

潘守護霊　うーん……秘密の使命？（笑）　秘密の使命なんてないよ。私の使命はきわめて明快で、日本による危険な未来を食い止めることです。安倍さんは、「日本が帰ってきた」と言ったけど、どういう意味なんだろうね？　日本が帰ってきたって？　「スーパーマンが帰ってきた」というタイトルなら知ってるけど。

石川　日本が新たな世界のリーダーになるという意味です。

潘守護霊　日本がまた軍事力を強めて、軍事大国になりた

and become a great military power again? Or, Japan wants to fight against China again? Or, Japan also wants to fight against North Korea and South Korea? Is that the meaning?

**Ishikawa**  We are trying to contain North Korea and China.

**Ban's G.S.**  Contain? No, no, no. China is a much greater country. You cannot. It's impossible! Please think about yourself only. Your problems, your inside problems only.

**Ishikawa**  You said it yourself that China has a lot of human rights problems, right?

**Ban's G.S.**  War shrine. I'm talking about the war shrine. Please destroy your war shrine.

がっているということか？　それとも、日本はまた中国と戦いたいということか？　あるいは、日本は北朝鮮や韓国とも戦いたいということか？　そういうことか？

石川　私たちは、北朝鮮と中国を封じ込めようとしているんです。

潘守護霊　封じ込める？　いやいやいや。中国はずうっと大きな国だよ。君たちには無理だ。不可能だ！　自分たちのことだけ考えていなさい。自分たちの問題、内部の問題だけ。

石川　あなたご自身もおっしゃったではないですか。中国は、人権問題を数多く抱えているわけですよね。

潘守護霊　戦争神社だ。戦争神社のことだよ。ぜひとも、君たちの戦争神社を取り壊してほしい。

## 19 Mr. Abe Should Destroy Yasukuni Shrine

**Ishikawa**  No, no. Compared to China, Japan is a very peaceful country.

**Ban's G.S.**  That would be helpful for world peace. Mr. Abe should destroy the war shrine, Yasukuni Shrine. That will let all people of the world free from the dangers of the next world war.

**Ichikawa**  But the Yasukuni problem is just our matter. It's not your matter.

**Ban's G.S.**  Not "your matter"? You should change. You should tackle your own matter. You should live in Japanese territory only. Never get out from Japan again!

石川　いえいえ、中国に比べたら、日本はとても平和な国です。

潘守護霊　そうすれば、世界平和の助けになるよ。安倍さんは、戦争神社、靖国(やすくに)神社を取り壊すべきです。そうすれば、世界中の人が皆(みんな)、次の世界大戦の危機から自由になれるというものだ。

市川　ですが、靖国問題は単に私たちの問題です。あなたたちの問題ではありません。

潘守護霊　「あなたたちの問題」ではない？　君たちは変わらないといかんな。君たち自身の問題に取り組まないといかん。日本の領土の中でだけ生きてなさいよ。二度と日本から外に出てくるな！

# 20 We Will Never Forgive Japanese People

**Ichikawa**  Thinking about China...

**Ban's G.S.**  China is a greater country.

**Ichikawa**  Did Mr. Xi Jinping ask you to do something that would benefit them?

**Ban's G.S.**  "Please follow me," he said. That's all.

**Ichikawa**  Ah-ha. So, you agreed? Are you going to follow his guidance?

**Ban's G.S.**  Of course. China will be the next greatest country in the near future, in the next 10 years. So, South Korea should obey China. America is sinking into the dark sea.

## 20　我々は決して日本人を許さない

市川　中国のことを考えてみると……。

**潘守護霊**　中国は、ずっと大きな国だ。

市川　習近平氏はあなたに、何か彼らの利益になるようなことを依頼しましたか。

**潘守護霊**　「私についてきてください」と言ってたな。それだけだよ。

市川　なるほど。それで、あなたは同意したのですか。あなたは彼の指導に従うということでしょうか。

**潘守護霊**　当然だろう。中国は、ここ 10 年くらいの近い将来、世界の次の最強国になるんだからさ。だから、韓国は中国に従わないといけない。アメリカは、暗い海に沈もうとしているんだから。

**Ishikawa**  But the Great East Asia War in World War II, in Japanese we call it *Daitoa Sensou*, was a kind of a holy war to emancipate our fellow brothers.

**Ban's G.S.**  For Japanese only.

**Ishikawa**  For Asian countries. Do you know that Japan put forth the Racial Equality Proposal when the League of Nations was being established? We insisted that. Every nation...

**Ban's G.S.**  We suffered a lot from Japanese intrusion. So...

**Ishikawa**  No, no, no, no.

**Ban's G.S.**  Japanese people are evil by nature.

**Ishikawa**  No. For example, the father of Current President Park felt grateful for Japan. Japan offered a

20　我々は決して日本人を許さない

石川　でも、第二次世界大戦の大東亜戦争、日本語では大東亜戦争と呼んでいるのですが、それは友邦を解放するための、一種の聖戦でした。

**潘守護霊**　日本のためだけだよ。

石川　アジア諸国のためだったんです。日本が国際連盟設立の際に人種的差別撤廃提案を出したことをご存じですか。私たちは主張したのです。すべての国の……。

**潘守護霊**　私たちは日本の侵略によって非常に苦しめられた。だから……。

石川　いえ、いえ、いえ、いえ。

**潘守護霊**　日本人は生まれながらに邪悪なんだ。

石川　いいえ、例えば、現在の朴大統領のお父さんは、日本に対して感謝していました。日本は、優れた教育を

175

lot of good education.

**Ban's G.S.** He received education from Japan and...

**Ishikawa** Yes, yes, he also studied Japanese.

**Ban's G.S.** That destroyed the natural laws of South Korea.

**Ishikawa** He was very poor so he must not have had a chance to study or for academics.

**Ban's G.S.** But he, himself, in himself, hated Japanese. Japanese people are very snobby people and they look down upon Korean people. They said "Korean people are pig-like people." They thought like that. We will never forgive you! Ohh, these are just the words of the guardian spirit so it's not the opinion of Mr. Ban.

たくさん提供しましたから。

**潘守護霊** 彼は日本から教育を受けて……。

**石川** はい、そうです、日本語も勉強しました。

**潘守護霊** それが韓国の自然法を破壊したんだ。

**石川** 彼は非常に貧しかったから、勉強する機会、学問の機会がなかったはずなんです。

**潘守護霊** だが彼自身は、彼の中では、日本人を憎んでいたぞ。日本人は上流気取りで、韓国人を見下している。「韓国人はブタのような人間たちだ」と言って、そう思ってたんだからな。我々は決して、お前たちを許さない！おお、これは単なる守護霊の言葉で、潘氏の意見じゃないからね。

**Ishikawa** But when Former Prime Minister Fukuda visited South Korea and at that time, Former President Park's cabinet members criticized Japan, Mr. Park stopped that. He said not to speak ill of Japan.

**Ban's G.S.** OK, OK, OK, OK, OK, OK.

**Ishikawa** Japanese regime was not so bad.

**Ban's G.S.** If you think so…

**Ishikawa** No, no, that's the story according to the cabinet official who was there at the time.

**Ban's G.S.** Please call the former president Mr. Park. Please summon him instead of me. So that's your conclusion, right? I think so.

**石川**　でも、朴大統領のお父さんは、福田元首相が韓国を訪れた時に、彼の閣僚たちが日本を批判したら、それを止めています。日本を悪く言うのはやめなさいと。

**潘守護霊**　分かった、分かった、分かった、分かった、分かった、分かった。

**石川**　日本の統治は、それほど悪くはなかったんです。

**潘守護霊**　そう思うんだったら……。

**石川**　いえ、いえ、その場にいた日本の閣僚が直接聞いた話です。

**潘守護霊**　元大統領の朴氏を呼んでください。私の代わりに、彼を招霊してください。それが君の結論だろう？　そう思うよ。

# 21 Past Life: Gandhi, Christ or Buddha?

**Ichikawa**  Thank you very much, Mr. Guardian Spirit. Time is up so I want to ask you the last question.

**Ban's G.S.**  Oh, lucky, lucky. It's over.

**Ichikawa**  Last question. As a guardian spirit, do you remember? Do you remember your past life?

**Ban's G.S.**  Past life?

**Ichikawa**  Past life of Mr. Ban.

**Ban's G.S.**  Maybe Mahatma Gandhi or Jesus Christ. Or Buddha, maybe.

**Ichikawa**  That's impossible.

## 21　過去世は「ガンジーかキリストか仏陀」？

**市川**　守護霊様、ありがとうございます。時間が来ましたので最後の質問をしたいと思います。

**潘守護霊**　おー、ラッキー、ラッキー。終わりだ。

**市川**　最後の質問です。守護霊として、あなたは記憶がありますか。ご自分の過去世(かこぜ)を覚えていますか。

**潘守護霊**　過去世？

**市川**　潘氏の過去世です。

**潘守護霊**　もしかするとマハトマ・ガンジーかイエス・キリストかも。あるいは、仏陀かもしれない。

**市川**　ありえません。

## 21 Past Life: Gandhi, Christ or Buddha?

**Ban's G.S.**  No, it's possible.

**Ichikawa**  Please remember your past life.

**Ban's G.S.**  If Buddha, Jesus Christ or Mahatma Gandhi was reborn in South Korea, he would become the secretary-general of the U.N. (hits table) Muhahahahaha.

**Oikawa**  Mr. Guardian Spirit, do you have any memory of when you descended to the earth, wore the physical body and lived a life on earth?

**Ban's G.S.**  Hmm...

**Oikawa**  Do you have any memory?

**Ban's G.S.**  Hmm... memory.

**Oikawa**  When was it?

21 過去世は「ガンジーかキリストか仏陀」？

**潘守護霊** いや、ありうる。

**市川** どうぞ、ご自分の過去世を思い出してください。

**潘守護霊** もし、仏陀やイエス・キリストやマハトマ・ガンジーが韓国に生まれ変わったら、国連事務総長になるんじゃないかな。(机を叩き) ムハハハハハ。

**及川** 守護霊様、地上に降りて、肉体に宿って、地上で人生を生きたときの記憶は、何かありますか。

**潘守護霊** うーん……。

**及川** 何か覚えていますか。

**潘守護霊** うーん……記憶ねえ。

**及川** それはいつでしたか。

**Ban's G.S.**  Hmm… I have a memory regarding Buddhism, Christianity and Confucianism.

**Oikawa**  OK. In which country? China?

**Ban's G.S.**  I have a worldwide recognition so maybe I was born in a lot of countries.

**Oikawa**  OK, OK. If you were to choose one specific country.

**Ban's G.S.**  Specific country… hmm.

**Oikawa**  In which country do you have the most vivid memory?

**Ban's G.S.**  China, China, China, China, China, China, India, Egypt…

**Oikawa**  OK. What were you doing?

21 過去世は「ガンジーかキリストか仏陀」？

潘守護霊　うーん……仏教やキリスト教や儒教に関する記憶はあるんだけど。

及川　分かりました、どこの国ですか。中国？

潘守護霊　私は世界的に認知されているから、いろんな国に生まれていたのかもしれない。

及川　はいはい。具体的な国を選ぶとしたら。

潘守護霊　具体的な国……うーん。

及川　いちばん鮮明な記憶があるのはどこですか。

潘守護霊　中国、中国、中国、中国、中国、中国、インド、エジプト……。

及川　分かりました。何をしていましたか。

**Ban's G.S.** Huh?

**Oikawa** What were you doing?

**Ban's G.S.** Hmm... maybe a king or a priest.

**Oikawa** King or priest? Then, do your names still remain in history? Can we recognize your old names?

**Ban's G.S.** You know Jesus Christ. You know Buddha. You know Gandhi.

**Oikawa** Anything else?

**Ban's G.S.** That's all.

**Oikawa** OK. Again, in which country were you born (audience laughs)?

**Ishikawa** Are you a liar?

21　過去世は「ガンジーかキリストか仏陀」?

**潘守護霊**　はあ?

**及川**　何をしていましたか。

**潘守護霊**　うーん……。王様か聖職者かもね。

**及川**　王様か聖職者?　では、歴史に名前が遺っていますか。私たちに分かる名前でしょうか。

**潘守護霊**　イエス・キリストは知ってるだろう。仏陀も知ってるよね。ガンジーも分かるよね。

**及川**　他には。

**潘守護霊**　それだけだね。

**及川**　分かりました。もう一度お聞きしますが、どの国に生まれましたか(会場笑)。

**石川**　あなたは嘘つきですか。

## 21 Past Life: Gandhi, Christ or Buddha?

**Ban's G.S.** I'm a "secret general." There is a hidden story, too. Hidden story. I...

**Ichikawa** China? Were you in China? Do you have any memory of China? In a past life?

**Ban's G.S.** Yeah, yeah, yeah. Memory. Of course.

**Ishikawa** Maybe a bureaucrat?

**Ban's G.S.** Hmm... maybe a king.

**Oikawa** OK, OK. Which era?

**Ban's G.S.** (laughs)

**Oikawa** Which era?

**Ban's G.S.** Secret, secret.

潘守護霊　私は「秘密総長」だ。秘密の話もある。秘密の話だ。私は……。

市川　中国ですか。中国にいましたか。中国の記憶がありますか。過去世として。

潘守護霊　うん、うん、うん。記憶ね。もちろんあるよ。

石川　官僚とか。

潘守護霊　うーん……王様かも。

及川　はいはい。どの時代ですか。

潘守護霊　（笑）

及川　どの時代ですか。

潘守護霊　秘密、秘密。

**Ishikawa**  You are not a decision-maker, so you are not a king, I think.

**Ban's G.S.**  But I am the person of number one quality in South Korea. Everyone admits about that.

## 22 Guardian Spirit Insists He is Neutral; Next Mission is President of South Korea

**Oikawa**  OK. Then, before closing this interview, I have one more question, the last question. OK? We understand that you hate Mr. Abe, but before you became a...

**Ban's G.S.**  Oh, Mr. Abe! Oh... (looks unpleasant)

**Oikawa**  OK, OK. OK, OK. OK. So before you became the secretary-general, you developed a

石川　あなたは意思決定者ではありませんから、王様ではないと思います。

潘守護霊　でも、私は韓国で、いちばん優秀な人間だ。それは誰もが認めるところだからな。

## 22　あくまで「中立」を主張。次の使命は「韓国大統領」

及川　分かりました。では、インタビューを終える前に、最後にもう一つ質問があります。よろしいですか。あなたは安倍さんを嫌っていると我々は理解しています。しかし、あなたが以前……。

潘守護霊　おお、安倍さん！　おお（嫌そうな表情を浮かべる）。

及川　はいはい、はいはい、はい。それで、事務総長になる前に、あなたは、麻生さんと個人的な人間関係を、

personal relationship or trust with Mr. Aso.

**Ban's G.S.** Aso…

**Oikawa** The current Japanese vice prime minister. Because of Mr. Aso's help, Japan helped you to become the secretary-general. What kind of relationship do you have with Mr. Aso? Or did you just use him?

**Ban's G.S.** Hmm… Mr. Aso. I don't like him. But he is a Christian. He's a Christian. He can speak English, a little. So I've been keeping good company with him. But my real intention is quite different from his. He, himself, must have a dictator tendency in him, like Abe. Japanese religion must be stopped. Now, Ise Shrine is collecting a lot of money so…

**Oikawa** Do you expect Mr. Aso to become the next Japanese prime minister after Mr. Abe?

信頼を築きましたよね。

**潘守護霊** 麻生か……。

**及川** 現在の日本の副総理です。麻生さんの支援のおかげで、日本はあなたが事務総長になる手助けをしました。麻生さんとはどのようなご関係ですか。それとも、彼を利用しただけですか。

**潘守護霊** うーん……。麻生さんね。好きじゃないな。でも、彼はクリスチャンだ。クリスチャンなんだ。英語も少し話せる。だから、彼とは仲良くしてる。でも、私の本心は彼とは全然違うからね。彼は、彼自身は、独裁者的な傾向を内面に持っているはずだよ。安倍みたいにね。日本の宗教はやめさせないといかんわなあ。今、伊勢神宮がたくさんお金を集めているから……。

**及川** あなたは、麻生さんが、安倍さんのあと、次の日本の総理大臣になることを期待していますか。

**Ban's G.S.**  Ahh… that's a disaster, too. Mr. Abe is a world disaster and Aso is, also (clicks tongue). They are thinking very bad things because their ancestors were bad people. They (ancestors) must be in Hell now, I guess.

**Ishikawa**  OK. OK. You don't have a neutral stance. We know very well.

**Ban's G.S.**  No, I'm neutral. I'm neutral.

**Ishikawa**  No, one-sided person. OK.

**Ban's G.S.**  I'm neutral.

**Ichikawa**  Thank you very much.

**Ban's G.S.**  But please choose the next secretary-general from the Japanese, if any country agrees with that conclusion. It's OK.

22　あくまで「中立」を主張。次の使命は「韓国大統領」

**潘守護霊**　あああ……そりゃあ、また災難だな。安倍さんは世界的な災難だし、麻生もそうだ（舌打ち）。彼らは非常に悪いことを考えている。何しろ、先祖が悪人だったからな。彼ら（先祖）は、きっと地獄にいると思うよ。

**石川**　はい、分かりました。あなたは中立的な立場をとっていませんね。非常によく分かりました。

**潘守護霊**　いや、私は中立だ。中立だよ。

**石川**　いいえ、偏った人です。分かりました。

**潘守護霊**　中立です。

**市川**　ありがとうございました。

**潘守護霊**　でも、次の事務総長は、どうぞ日本人から選んでくれたまえ。もし、その決定に賛成する国があるならね。構いませんから。

**Ishikawa**  Would you support Japan?

**Ban's G.S.**  No, of course not. But if that's possible, it's OK.

**Ichikawa**  After you resign as the secretary-general, what would you do? What's your next mission? Work for South Korea?

**Ban's G.S.**  My next mission? Ah, it's the president of South Korea.

**Ichikawa**  You want to be the president of South Korea?

**Ban's G.S.**  Yeah. I will be.

**Ichikawa**  Thank you very much.

## 22　あくまで「中立」を主張。次の使命は「韓国大統領」

石川　あなたは日本を支持しますか。

潘守護霊　いや、する訳ないでしょう。でも、それが可能なら構いませんよ。

市川　あなたは事務総長を辞めたあと、何をしようと思っていますか。次なる使命は何ですか。韓国のために働きますか。

潘守護霊　私の次なる使命？　そりゃあ、韓国の大統領ですよ。

市川　韓国の大統領になりたいのですか。


潘守護霊　うん、なるよ。

市川　どうもありがとうございました。

**Ishikawa**  This concludes today's session. Thank you so much.

**Ban's G.S.**  Thank you very much.

# 23 After the Interview with the Guardian Spirit of U.N. Secretary-General Ban

**Ryuho Okawa**  Ahh, he's not a mediocrat person. I think it's some kind of a mistake. South Korea has a one-sided opinion regarding Japanese matters, so he's not the right person, I think.

I wish for the next secretary-general to be a neutral person. The next secretary-general should be the right person who can handle the China-Japan problem and of course the Korea-Japan problem, and also the person who can adjust the Israel and Islam people problem. It might be very difficult.

But maybe, I guess, the next secretary-general

石川　これで本日の収録を終わります。ありがとうございました。

潘守護霊　どうもありがとう。

# 23　「潘国連事務総長の守護霊インタビュー」を終えて

大川隆法　ああ、彼は中程度の人物でもありませんね。何かの間違いだと思います。韓国は日本との問題に関して、偏った意見を持っていますので、彼は適任者ではないと思います。

　次の事務総長は中立的な人であることを願いたいものです。次の事務総長は、日中問題や、もちろん日韓問題に対処できる適任者であり、イスラエルとイスラムの人々の問題を調整できる人であるべきでしょうね。非常に難しいことかもしれませんが。

　私の推測では次の事務総長は、インド系の人や、ある

should be an Indian-like person or person from a smaller country than India, and that person should have various values regarding a lot of matters. He who has various values can be a neutral person. I think so.

So his mission is already almost finished, I think. Lately, this August, he accused of the Japanese history recognition, but he forgot to be neutral as the secretary-general of the U.N. So, he can't be another nationality. He, himself, is a Korean person. He didn't say anything about his past life, but I guess his last past life must have been Korean. That's all.

## 23 「潘国連事務総長の守護霊インタビュー」を終えて

いはインドより小さい国の人で、多くの問題に関して多様な価値観を持った人物であるべきです。多様な価値観を持っている人物であれば、中立であることができると思います。

　彼のミッションは、すでにほぼ終わっているようですね。最近、この８月に、彼は日本の歴史認識を非難しましたが、国連事務総長としての中立性を忘れていました。彼は別の国籍になることなどできません。彼自身は韓国人です。過去世については何も言いませんでしたが、おそらく直前世も韓国人だったに違いないと思います。以上です。

潘基文国連事務総長の守護霊インタビュー

2013年10月24日　初版第1刷

著　者　　大川隆法

発行所　　幸福の科学出版株式会社

〒107-0052　東京都港区赤坂2丁目10番14号
TEL(03)5573-7700
http://www.irhpress.co.jp/

印刷・製本　　株式会社 堀内印刷所

落丁・乱丁本はおとりかえいたします
©Ryuho Okawa 2013. Printed in Japan. 検印省略
ISBN978-4-86395-403-8 C0030
Photo：AP/アフロ

## 大川隆法ベストセラーズ・希望の未来を切り拓く

# 未来の法
### 新たなる地球世紀へ

暗い世相に負けるな！ 悲観的な自己像に縛られるな！ 心に眠る無限のパワーに目覚めよ！ 人類の未来を拓く鍵は、一人ひとりの心のなかにある。

2,000円

# 救世の法
### 信仰と未来社会

信仰を持つことの功徳や、民族・宗教対立を終わらせる考え方など、人類への希望が示される。地球神の説くほんとうの「救い」とは──。

1,800円

# 国を守る宗教の力
### この国に正論と正義を

3年前から国防と経済の危機を警告してきた国師が、迷走する日本を一喝！ 国難を打破し、日本を復活させる正論を訴える。
【幸福実現党刊】

1,500円

幸福の科学出版

## 大川隆法 ベストセラーズ・世界で活躍する宗教家の本音

## 大川隆法の守護霊霊言
### ユートピア実現への挑戦

あの世の存在証明による霊性革命、正論と神仏の正義による政治革命。幸福の科学グループ創始者兼総裁の本心が、ついに明かされる。

1,400円

---

## 政治革命家・大川隆法
### 幸福実現党の父

未来が見える。嘘をつかない。タブーに挑戦する──。政治の問題を鋭く指摘し、具体的な打開策を唱える幸福実現党の魅力が分かる万人必読の書。

1,400円

---

## 素顔の大川隆法

素朴な疑問からドキッとするテーマまで、女性編集長3人の質問に気さくに答えた、101分公開ロングインタビュー。大注目の宗教家が、その本音を明かす。

1,300円

※表示価格は本体価格(税別)です。

## 大川隆法ベストセラーズ・エル・カンターレの基本三法

# 太陽の法
### エル・カンターレへの道

創世記や愛の段階、悟りの構造、文明の流転を明快に説き、主エル・カンターレの真実の使命を示した、仏法真理の基本書。

2,000円

---

# 黄金の法
### エル・カンターレの歴史観

歴史上の偉人たちの活躍を鳥瞰しつつ、隠されていた人類の秘史を公開し、人類の未来をも予言した、空前絶後の人類史。

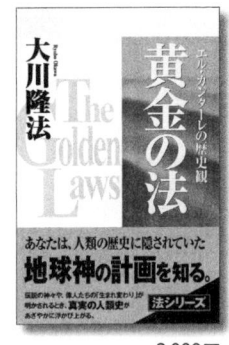

2,000円

---

# 永遠の法
### エル・カンターレの世界観

『太陽の法』(法体系)、『黄金の法』(時間論)に続いて、本書は空間論を開示し、次元構造など、霊界の真の姿を明確に説き明かす。

2,000円

幸福の科学出版

## 大川隆法 ベストセラーズ・英語説法＆最新英語霊言

### Power to the Future
**未来に力を**

英語説法集 日本語訳付き

予断を許さない日本の国防危機。混迷を極める世界情勢の行方——。ワールド・ティーチャーが英語で語った、この国と世界の進むべき道とは。

1,400円

---

### アサド大統領の スピリチュアル・メッセージ

英語霊言 日本語訳付き

混迷するシリア問題の真相を探るため、アサド大統領の守護霊霊言に挑む——。恐るべき独裁者の実像が明らかに！

1,400円

---

### マザー・テレサの 宗教観を伝える
**神と信仰、この世と来世、そしてミッション**

英語霊言 日本語訳付き

神の声を聞き、貧しい人びとを救うために、その生涯を捧げた高名な修道女マザー・テレサ——。いま、ふたたび「愛の言葉」を語りはじめる。

1,400円

※表示価格は本体価格（税別）です。

## 大川隆法霊言シリーズ・霊言で読む国際情勢

### バラク・オバマの
### スピリチュアル・メッセージ
**再選大統領は世界に平和をもたらすか**

弱者救済と軍事費削減、富裕層への増税……。再選翌日のオバマ大統領守護霊インタビューを緊急刊行！日本の国防危機が明らかになる。
【幸福実現党刊】

英語霊言
日本語訳付き

1,400円

---

### サッチャーの
### スピリチュアル・メッセージ
**死後19時間での奇跡のインタビュー**

フォークランド紛争、英国病、景気回復……。勇気を持って数々の難問を解決し、イギリスを繁栄に導いたサッチャー元首相が、日本にアドバイス！

英語霊言
日本語訳付き

1,300円

---

### ロシア・プーチン
### 新大統領と帝国の未来
**守護霊インタヴュー**

中国が覇権主義を拡大させるなか、ロシアはどんな国家戦略をとるのか!? また、親日家プーチン氏の意外な過去世も明らかに。
【幸福実現党刊】

1,300円

幸福の科学出版

## 大川隆法霊言シリーズ・韓国と北朝鮮の真実

### 安重根は韓国の英雄か、それとも悪魔か
#### 安重根 & 朴槿惠大統領守護霊の霊言

なぜ韓国は、中国にすり寄るのか？ 従軍慰安婦の次は、安重根像の設置を打ち出す朴槿惠・韓国大統領の恐るべき真意が明らかに。

1,400円

---

### 神に誓って「従軍慰安婦」は実在したか

いまこそ、「歴史認識」というウソの連鎖を断つ！ 元従軍慰安婦を名乗る2人の守護霊インタビューを刊行！ 慰安婦問題に隠された驚くべき陰謀とは⁉
【幸福実現党刊】

1,400円

---

### 北朝鮮の未来透視に挑戦する
#### エドガー・ケイシー リーディング

「第2次朝鮮戦争」勃発か⁉ 核保有国となった北朝鮮と、その挑発に乗った韓国が激突。地獄に堕ちた建国の父〟金日成の霊言も同時収録。

1,400円

※表示価格は本体価格（税別）です。

## 大川隆法 霊言シリーズ・正しい歴史認識のために

### 公開霊言 東條英機、「大東亜戦争の真実」を語る

戦争責任、靖国参拝、憲法改正……。
他国からの不当な内政干渉にモノ言
えぬ日本。正しい歴史認識を求めて、
東條英機が先の大戦の真相を語る。
【幸福実現党刊】

1,400円

### 原爆投下は人類への罪か？
#### 公開霊言 トルーマン ＆ F・ルーズベルトの新証言

なぜ、終戦間際に、アメリカは日本
に2度も原爆を落としたのか？「憲
法改正」を語る上で避けては通れ
ない難題に「公開霊言」が挑む。
【幸福実現党刊】

1,400円

### 「河野談話」「村山談話」を斬る！
#### 日本を転落させた歴史認識

根拠なき歴史認識で、これ以上日本
が謝る必要などない!! 守護霊イン
タビューで明らかになった、驚愕の新
証言。「大川談話（私案）」も収録。

1,400円

幸福の科学出版

## 大川隆法霊言シリーズ・中東問題の真相に迫る

### イラン大統領 vs. イスラエル首相
**中東の核戦争は回避できるのか**

世界が注視するイランとイスラエルの対立。それぞれのトップの守護霊が、緊迫する中東問題の核心を赤裸々に語る。
【幸福実現党刊】

1,400円

---

### イラク戦争は正しかったか
**サダム・フセインの死後を霊査する**

全世界衝撃の公開霊言。「大量破壊兵器は存在した!」「9.11はフセインが計画し、ビン・ラディンが実行した!」——。驚愕の事実が明らかに。

1,400円

---

### イスラム過激派に正義はあるのか
**オサマ・ビン・ラディンの霊言に挑む**

「アルジェリア人質事件」の背後には何があるのか——。死後も暗躍を続ける、オサマ・ビン・ラディンが語った「戦慄の事実」。

1,400円

※表示価格は本体価格(税別)です。

# 幸福の科学グループのご案内

**宗教、教育、政治、出版などの活動を通じて、地球的ユートピアの実現を目指しています。**

## 宗教法人 幸福の科学

　一九八六年に立宗。一九九一年に宗教法人格を取得。信仰の対象は、地球系霊団の最高大霊、主エル・カンターレ。世界百カ国以上の国々に信者を持ち、全人類救済という尊い使命のもと、信者は、「愛」と「悟り」と「ユートピア建設」の教えの実践、伝道に励んでいます。

（二〇二三年十月現在）

## 愛

幸福の科学の「愛」とは、与える愛です。これは、仏教の慈悲や布施の精神と同じことです。信者は、仏法真理をお伝えすることを通して、多くの方に幸福な人生を送っていただくための活動に励んでいます。

## 悟り

「悟り」とは、自らが仏の子であることを知るということです。教学や精神統一によって心を磨き、智慧を得て悩みを解決すると共に、天使・菩薩の境地を目指し、より多くの人を救える力を身につけていきます。

## ユートピア建設

私たち人間は、地上に理想世界を建設するという尊い使命を持って生まれてきています。社会の悪を押しとどめ、善を推し進めるために、信者はさまざまな活動に積極的に参加しています。

### 海外支援・災害支援

国内外の世界で貧困や災害、心の病で苦しんでいる人々に対しては、現地メンバーや支援団体と連携して、物心両面にわたり、あらゆる手段で手を差し伸べています。

年間約3万人の自殺者を減らすため、全国各地で街頭キャンペーンを展開しています。

公式サイト **www.withyou-hs.net**

### ヘレンの会

ヘレン・ケラーを理想として活動する、ハンディキャップを持つ方とボランティアの会です。視聴覚障害者、肢体不自由な方々に仏法真理を学んでいただくための、さまざまなサポートをしています。

公式サイト **www.helen-hs.net**

---

**INFORMATION**

お近くの精舎・支部・拠点など、お問い合わせは、こちらまで！
幸福の科学サービスセンター
TEL. **03-5793-1727** (受付時間 火～金:10～20時／土・日:10～18時)
宗教法人 幸福の科学 公式サイト **happy-science.jp**

## 教育

## 学校法人 幸福の科学学園

学校法人 幸福の科学学園は、幸福の科学の教育理念のもとにつくられた教育機関です。人間にとって最も大切な宗教教育の導入を通じて精神性を高めながら、ユートピア建設に貢献する人材輩出を目指しています。

**幸福の科学学園**
**中学校・高等学校（那須本校）**
2010年4月開校・栃木県那須郡（男女共学・全寮制）
TEL 0287-75-7777
公式サイト happy-science.ac.jp

**関西中学校・高等学校（関西校）**
2013年4月開校・滋賀県大津市（男女共学・寮及び通学）
TEL 077-573-7774
公式サイト kansai.happy-science.ac.jp

**幸福の科学大学**（仮称・設置認可申請予定）
2015年開学予定
TEL 03-6277-7248（幸福の科学 大学準備室）
公式サイト university.happy-science.jp

### 仏法真理塾「サクセスNo.1」
小・中・高校生が、信仰教育を基礎にしながら、「勉強も『心の修行』」と考えて学んでいます。
TEL 03-5750-0747（東京本校）

### 不登校児支援スクール「ネバー・マインド」
心の面からのアプローチを重視して、不登校の子供たちを支援しています。
また、障害児支援の「ユー・アー・エンゼル!」運動も行っています。
TEL 03-5750-1741

### エンゼルプランV
幼少時からの心の教育を大切にして、信仰をベースにした幼児教育を行っています。
TEL 03-5750-0757

### NPO 活動支援
学校からのいじめ追放を目指し、さまざまな社会提言をしています。また、各地でのシンポジウムや学校への啓発ポスター掲示等に取り組むNPO「いじめから子供を守ろう！ネットワーク」を支援しています。
公式サイト mamoro.org
ブログ mamoro.blog86.fc2.com
相談窓口 TEL.03-5719-2170

## 政治

### 幸福実現党

内憂外患(ないゆうがいかん)の国難に立ち向かうべく、二〇〇九年五月に幸福実現党を立党しました。創立者である大川隆法総裁の精神的指導のもと、宗教だけでは解決できない問題に取り組み、幸福を具体化するための力になっています。

党員の機関紙「幸福実現NEWS」

**TEL** 03-6441-0754
**公式サイト** hr-party.jp

## 出版メディア事業

### 幸福の科学出版

大川隆法総裁の仏法真理の書を中心に、ビジネス、自己啓発、小説など、さまざまなジャンルの書籍・雑誌を出版しています。他にも、映画事業、文学・学術発展のための振興事業、テレビ・ラジオ番組の提供など、幸福の科学文化を広げる事業を行っています。

**TEL** 03-5573-7700
**公式サイト** irhpress.co.jp

# 入 会 の ご 案 内

## あなたも、幸福の科学に集い、ほんとうの幸福を見つけてみませんか？

幸福の科学では、大川隆法総裁が説く仏法真理をもとに、
「どうすれば幸福になれるのか、また、
他の人を幸福にできるのか」を学び、実践しています。

### 入会

大川隆法総裁の教えを信じ、学ぼうとする方なら、どなたでも入会できます。入会された方には、『入会版「正心法語」』が授与されます。（入会の奉納は1,000円目安です）

**ネットでも入会**できます。詳しくは、下記URLへ。
**happy-science.jp/joinus**

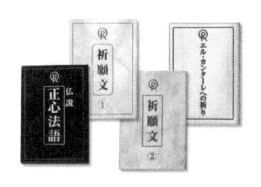

### 三帰誓願 (さんきせいがん)

仏弟子としてさらに信仰を深めたい方は、仏・法・僧の三宝への帰依を誓う「三帰誓願式」を受けることができます。三帰誓願者には、『仏説・正心法語』『祈願文①』『祈願文②』『エル・カンターレへの祈り』が授与されます。

### 植福の会 (しょくふくのかい)

植福は、ユートピア建設のために、自分の富を差し出す尊い布施の行為です。布施の機会として、毎月1口1,000円からお申込みいただける、「植福の会」がございます。

月刊「幸福の科学」
ザ・伝道

「植福の会」に参加された方のうちご希望の方には、幸福の科学の小冊子（毎月1回）をお送りいたします。詳しくは、下記の電話番号までお問い合わせください。

ヤング・ブッダ
ヘルメス・エンゼルズ

---

**INFORMATION**
**幸福の科学サービスセンター**
**TEL. 03-5793-1727**（受付時間 火～金:10～20時／土・日:10～18時)
宗教法人 幸福の科学 公式サイト **happy-science.jp**